I Lived
To Tell
About It!

By
Joey Perez

www.worldevangmin.org

I Lived to Tell About It!

Published by Worldwide Evangelistic Ministries, Inc.
P. O. Box 46496
Philadelphia, PA 19160-6496
(215) 223-1022 / (215) 223-1916

Unless otherwise noted, all Scripture quotations are from the New King James Version of the Bible. Copyright © 1979, 1980, 1982 by Thomas Nelson, Inc., publishers.

Cover design by Rick Wolfe
Edited by Weltha Wood
Proofread by Maxine Harris, Dave Cook, and Dr. Robert E. Brown

ISBN 978-0-9801064-0-4
Library of Congress Control Number: 2008922372

Printed in the United States of America

Dedication

I want to dedicate this book to my loving wife, Damaris, and our daughters, Christine and Ivellise. This book is also dedicated to my mother, Maria Rodriguez, who went to be with the Lord on October 20, 1990.

Foreword

By Pastor Frankie Cruz

The ministry of Philip the evangelist in the city of Samaria was one... [of the] acts of the apostles in which the Holy Ghost continued Jesus' work through the first century Church. At the beginning of the third millennium, Joey Perez's biography is another chapter to be added to the Acts of the Apostles. Pastor Joey Perez is one of the ministry gifts that our Lord has given to the Church. First of all, he is an urban evangelist, ready to preach the Gospel to every creature, but he is very effective among the drug addicts, alcoholics, gangs, law offenders, and those with life-controlling problems.

We (my wife Maria and I) were called to plant a church in the city of Las Piedras, Puerto Rico. We decided to go in our first week of community outreach to call out the members of The Rock Christian Center. Since we needed laborers to help us during this process, I went to the Assemblies of God Bible College in Bayamon for them. I was rejoicing in the Lord because the director, Reverend Carlos Osorio, had selected three of the best students for the activity. On my way out of the director's office, I heard from the next room a voice that cried aloud and sounded like a trumpet. I stopped and told the director, "I want to have that man in Las Piedras." That voice like a trumpet was Joey Perez. Joey Perez's story is an evangelistic message. You will share his tears as you read about the dark environment of gangs, drugs, violence, and crime in which he was raised, but you will rejoice because where sin abounded, grace did much more abound. He was raised from the dust, and he is seated with the princes of his people. As a child of Abraham, he was called to be blessed and to be a blessing to many cities and many nations.

I have seen Joey Perez grow up in the Lord. He has been blessed with Damaris, a virtuous wife, and their beautiful daughters, Christine and Ivellise. They are the founders of Worldwide Evangelistic Ministries, establishing two rehabilitation centers for men and women, and have planted a powerful church in the city of Philadelphia. I praise our Lord for Pastors Joey and Damaris because I have no greater joy than to hear that my children walk in truth.

By reading this book, if you are unsaved, you will be reproved of sin and will receive the Gospel, which is the power of God for salvation; if you are a Christian, the Holy Ghost will give you a strong anointing to reach out to every creature in your community.

The Rock Christian Center, Las Piedras, P.R.

Foreword

By Bishop Valeriano Melendez

This book will light a living flame in your heart for the presence of God. Joey Perez opens his heart in a transparent way for the Body of Christ to come into a new relationship with their Savior, Jesus Christ. I must warn you: This is a dangerous and dynamic book. If you are comfortable and complacent and want to stay that way, don't even open this book!

**Founder of Soul Saving Station Evangelistic Center
Ahoskie, North Carolina**

Contents

Chapter 1

A Young Life of Crime

"You shot up all my drug money? Well, stand still because I'm gonna shoot *you* all up!" I shouted as I pulled a gun on one of my drug dealers. I was going to kill Izzy; he had cheated me out of money that he owed me — *my* money. I stood there on that street corner with my gun pulled out to shoot him.

Suddenly, I felt a tap on my shoulder. It had to be the cops! I quickly stuck the gun back in my pocket and turned around to see . . . an elderly woman with white hair.

"What do you want, old lady?" I screamed at her. Her face glowing, she handed me four small pieces of paper.

"What's this? Don't you see I'm ready to kill this guy?"

"Young man, those are *tracts*! I was in my church praying, and God told me to come to this corner because there was a young man here who He wanted to save!"

I began to argue with her. Why would God send her to me of all people? While snarling that I hated her, I crumpled up the four little tracts she had given me and threw them at her, hitting her right in the face with them.

Terrified, she turned to run away from me; I chased her across the street, screaming my hatred. Suddenly, she stopped and turned, looking at me as she spoke: "Jesus loves you!"

As she spoke those words, my body flew backward. Once more, I told her I hated her. She responded the same as before, using that name, and again I flew backward. I stopped threatening this small, white-haired woman; instead, I began to shake, my entire body trembling with fear as I made my way home.

Home in North Philly

The farthest back I can remember is 1963, when I was six-years-old and my family lived at 2232 N. Second Street in Philadelphia, Pennsylvania. An Irish woman, Mrs. Hagherty, was frequently our babysitter. She had three Sons and three daughters. I envied her youngest son, Patrick, because it seemed to me that he always had everything he wanted. However, he was not greedy and shared his toys with us. Mrs. Hagherty's three daughters, all in their twenties, were beautiful, and even though I was only six, I was in love with two of them. One of them was Judith, and my mother named my youngest sister, Wanda Judith, after her; the others were Virginia and Veronica. I was in love with both Virginia and Judith because they constantly showed me so much love. Every time I went to their house, they would hug and kiss me and play games with me.

I remember that when I started first grade I was sick one day. My mother had left my brothers, Willie and Edwin, my sisters, Wandy, Debbie, and Vivian, and me with Mrs. Hagherty. There were ten children in my family at the time, four that were older than I was and five that were younger. We were on the floor at Mrs. Hagherty's watching President John F. Kennedy's motorcar procession go through the streets of Dallas on the television when suddenly the television went blank. I could hear Bill, Mrs. Hagherty's oldest son, yelling that the president had just been shot. I didn't understand what was going on. There was a big commotion, and Mrs. Hagherty and her daughters began to cry. I asked them what was wrong, but they would not answer. Because I didn't understand what was going on, I didn't ask any more questions.

At home one day soon after the assassination, I saw my mother crying and asked her, "Mommy, what's wrong?" After the president was killed, I frequently saw my mother crying, and I would ask her, "Mommy, why do you cry?"

8

Without answering me, she would simply look out the window, crying even more. Finally, one day she told me she was crying because the president was dead. But something deep inside me told me she was crying because my father was unfaithful to her.

My father had a good job as a residential building contractor. Sometimes, however, when he came home, he would beat my mother when she asked him about other women. I saw this but couldn't fully understand what was happening, and I felt terribly sorry for my mother. Even though my father was well paid in his job, my mother would often have to get up very early and stand in the surplus food line because we didn't have enough food for ten people; my father spent the money on other women.

Second Street was in a mixed neighborhood, predominately Irish and Polish with a few Chinese families and two Hispanic families: one Puerto Rican family with a little boy named Willie and our family. One of the Chinese boys was named Harry. He was a chubby little kid who was bigger than my brother Mikey (who was a year older than I) and me. On one occasion, Harry tried to bully us. We ran away, but he chased after us. We ran up to my house, and Mikey went inside the house while I stood outside cursing at Harry. When Mikey came back out, he had a fork, and he threw it at Harry. I watched as it spun a few times in the air before it stuck into Harry's head. He ran home screaming with that fork sticking out of his head.

Harry's mother came outside yelling something at us in Chinese; of course, we didn't understand what she was saying. My older brother Philip and our sister Evelyn came out of the house and began to yell back at her. This quickly turned into a screaming match between the two families. Someone called the police. When they arrived, they talked to my parents, and Mikey and I were punished. First, our parents whipped us, and then we had to stay in our rooms. But Mikey and I laughed about it the entire time because we

9

thought it was so funny.

I also remember a black woman in our neighborhood, Mrs. Jones, who had a number of children. She lived on Second and Dolphin Streets. She was a religious woman who also had beautiful daughters! I particularly remember one of them named Paulette. I was also in love with her because she was always hugging me and bringing us candy. Every now and then, Mrs. Jones would take us with her to her church. I remember going to the vacation Bible school there; I enjoyed drawing pictures. There were special pictures I could make by taking a pencil and scribbling across the paper; all of a sudden, a picture would appear. The pictures were of such things as Jesus holding little lambs.

A New Neighborhood

My father decided to move to 1849 Leithgow Street in 1964, when I was about seven-years-old. This neighborhood was predominantly German and Irish with a couple of Mongolian families. We were the only Hispanic family in the community at that time. I remember the children who lived on the corner, three brothers named Bobby, Joey, and Eddie. This family also had about ten children. They had another brother nicknamed Fats because he was quite chubby. He was heavily involved in sports.

Their brother Bobby wasn't; his interest lay in stealing. Bobby had a friend named David who lived around the corner. David's family was the only black family in that neighborhood at Fourth and Berks Streets. David and his brother Matthew stole from stores in downtown Philadelphia. As we became familiar with our neighbors, my older brother Philip became friends with Bobby, and they would frequently go downtown together to steal. I started hanging out with them, and Bobby showed me how to steal suits. We would go into Lit Brothers' and John

Wanamaker's. My friends would pretend that they were trying clothes on me. Instead, they would shove a couple pairs of trousers down my pants, put two suit jackets on me, put my own jacket on me, and walk me right out the door. People looking at me could not detect that I had stolen the suits.

Philip, Bobby, and I would then jump on the L (the elevated train) and take it to Mutter and Berks Streets. An Irish woman, Mrs. Green, ran a little candy store there. We would sell her the suits, and then she would sell them to someone else.

Little by little, after I found it was so easy to steal, I became used to it and even started to like it. Now and then, we would also go downtown to steal. When we weren't stealing, we played football with Bobby's brother and another boy named Kevin whose mother frequently sent me to the store and paid me a dime or even a quarter for going.

During this time, my family began to have serious problems at home. My parents fought with each other a great deal. My father and my mother worked so many hours that they left us by ourselves most of the time. My older sister Evelyn really couldn't take care of us. She was already a teenager and in love, spending her time with various friends. My sister's boyfriend would come over to the house, but I gave him my mean look and threw rocks at him so that he wouldn't come around anymore. We also had a friend whom I called Aunt. Her real name was Catalina Benjamin, and she had a daughter who used to live with us, in addition to the ten children already in our home. My sister Evelyn and Jackie Benjamin were the same age and so in love with boys that they were hardly ever around.

As it was, there was no peace in my house and no happiness either. My brothers and sisters and I were on our own. We stole, and after a while, we started sniffing glue. We bought toy car models just for the tube of glue inside. We moved on to smoking cigarettes and breaking into our neighbors' houses. David and his brother Matthew became such good thieves that they would go into suburban neighborhoods and rob people's houses, coming away with a great deal of money.

I had a cousin named Johnny who lived two doors away from David and Matthew. We used to go to Johnny's house, sneak out his third floor window onto the roof, and jump across roofs to David's house. From his backyard, we would break inside his house and take all the money he had stolen from someone else. We did this constantly.

I remember when I was only eight, I broke into his house while his oldest sister was downstairs watching television. I walked around on the second and third floors taking things I knew I could sell to buy glue. The room I focused on most was David's because I had heard him tell my friend Bobby that he had stolen quite a bit of money the day before.

Then I went into Matthew's room and found a hole in his mattress containing about nine hundred dollars. I took the money and gave it to Philip, telling him what had happened. I went out and bought myself some brand-new silk and wool pants and some double-knit shirts. That meant a lot to a kid my age because normally we couldn't afford anything like that. My father asked us where we were getting the money, and we told him that we had found it. He didn't question us anymore. He was hardly around any way; instead, he continued to run around with other women. He and my mother fought constantly.

There were times when my mother needed to buy food, but there wasn't any money because my father didn't give her any. To feed our family, she would go to the super market, taking us with her. I remember my mother always had a big purse, and as we walked through the store, she would pick out the things she was actually planning to buy. Whatever she couldn't pay for, she hid in her gigantic pocketbook. She would put toothpaste, ham, cheese, and a number of other items into her purse.

We would see her doing this, and we helped her out by putting other things in the back of our pants. Because we were wearing long coats, no one could see what we had taken. My mother did this because she didn't have enough money to buy the things she needed for twelve people. Out of ignorance, she was teaching us to steal, and I came to realize that she would pay a high price in the future.

When I was in the third grade, attending Moffet Elementary School on Second & Oxford, my friends and I played hooky. My parents did not even know this. It was a lot of fun living on Leithgow Street. Even though it was a mixed neighborhood, all of the kids pulled together. Sometimes Bobby, his brother Joey, my brothers, and I would have free-for-alls. We would separate into small groups and fight one another. But another person couldn't come into our neighborhood to start a fight or to bully us because everybody would join together — the Hispanics, the few black families, the Germans, the Irish, and the two Mongolian families. No one could come in to start anything because we would fight for our neighborhood and protect one another.

Even though we joined to fight others, there were many times when we fought among ourselves — family against family — the Perez family fighting the Acoffs, the Acoffs fighting the Bradys, the Bradys fighting a new black family that just moved in with six sons. Then we would all get together and fight people from other neighborhoods. After awhile, we considered ourselves to be the Leithgow and Berks gang. We used to hear all about the big gang wars that were going on in other neighborhoods. While we didn't have any real gang wars in our neighborhood, a little way up the street, on Eighth & Berks, in a predominantly black neighborhood, there was quite a bit of gang warfare. We heard about young men killing each other.

Meanwhile, we were busy learning how to steal, playing hooky from school, and getting into all kinds of trouble. My friends and I were locked up one time for breaking into our neighbor's house. I was only eight-years-old, but we were still taken to the police station. I cried and cried because I didn't want to be locked up. After awhile, I became used to it; the second time, when I was locked up for sniffing glue, it had already become easier to accept. This is how my life of crime started, living and being raised in North Philadelphia.

A Stabbing

One summer night in 1966 at three in the morning, when I was nine-years-old and still living on Leithgow Street, I heard my mother screaming. I looked out the window and saw that her nightgown was covered with blood. I watched her pull my father away from another man. I woke up Philip first and started yelling, "Mommy's cut! Mommy is bleeding!" All ten of us ran downstairs, and my sisters were screaming and crying. I could see that my father was also covered with blood. My father held a knife in his right hand and had just used it to stab a man in the side. Because our front door was broken, I thought that this man was a burglar who had tried to break into our house and that my father had caught him. I started to yell, "Pop, kill him! Pop, kill him!"

Soon the police swarmed over our entire neighborhood. At first, the police thought my mother was hurt, but she wasn't even cut. My father, however, had a broken head because the man had hit him on the head with a baseball bat. They had played pool earlier and made a bet. When my father won, the other man didn't pay him off. My father punched him, and the other guy showed up with the bat to beat my father, who used his knife in self-defense. The man had been stabbed seven or eight times. That night no one could sleep.

At first, my brothers and I bragged about Dad, saying, "Pop really did him in. Pop really did him in!" But the next day, we began to hear rumors that a number of men were coming to our house to kill my father. Mikey, Philip, my sister, and I took a bunch of milk bottles and filled them up with urine. We were quick; we knew how to get up on the roof in just a few seconds from the third floor of our house. We loaded the roof with bricks. That night we kept watch just to see if anyone was coming. If they had shown up, we were ready to throw bricks and milk bottles down on them from the roof. However, things calmed down.

My father had several friends who acted just as crazy as he did. He had a reputation for fighting, cutting, and shooting people. He didn't take anything from anyone. It seemed that every time we turned around, someone was looking for him because he had shot or knifed someone. Sometimes the cops came to our house looking for my father. I remember that a lot of people in our neighborhood didn't like us. They called us the big trouble family — a family with no peace. They were right.

During the time we lived on Leithgow Street, my mother would sit us in a circle and tell us stories about life on the island of Puerto Rico. Once she even told us that my father's mother was a witch who one day flew on a broom as many neighbors in the barrio watched. I believed her! She told us stories of people who had died and of people who were invisible. My mother and father believed in spiritualism, and my father practiced it. Because of this, there was no peace in our home. Frequently, we saw what appeared to be dark clouds and dark shadows running through our house, but we didn't really understand what was happening. We thought our house was haunted. My father lit candles to all kinds of gods and to the spirits of the Indians. He believed in this strongly but didn't know that he was

15

bringing all kinds of evil spirits into our house. Catalina Benjamin came to our house once and said she saw a black shadow in a flame of fire come into our house by crawling through the window. My mother saw snakes cross the ceiling one night as she lay in bed. Philip once saw a demon sitting with his legs crossed on the ledge of the high window between the bathroom and the bedroom.

I have many different memories from that time. I remember one day my father caught Philip and Mikey sniffing glue. While he didn't mind his sons drinking, he could not stand our sniffing glue or using drugs. He hit them on the head twice with a milk crate and beat them with an extension cord. Then he took a can, punched holes in it, and told Philip and Mikey to kneel down on it. When they were finally allowed to get up, their knees were covered with bloody holes. Then he stuck a sewing needle through their nose to further punish them for sniffing glue. I was glad I didn't get caught that time!

A black man named Mr. Fordham used to pick up my brothers and me and take us to the better neighborhoods. We had a printed card that we gave people to read. After they read it, they would ask us to come in because we had a bag full of all kinds of things: ashtrays, napkins, water pitchers, plastic cups, and anything else we could find to sell them. Finally, it looked as if we were making an honest dollar because we got to keep half of what we sold. Often these kind people would give us milk and cookies and sometimes sandwiches. But while they were in the kitchen getting us food, we looked around for things we could steal. We would put those things in our bags and leave. They never saw us again.

Chapter 2

Hanging with the Gangs

In the summer of 1967, my father decided to move again to Franklin and Berks Streets, only seven blocks away from Leithgow Street. This was a bad neighborhood with a lot of gang warfare going on. There were two well-known gangs in particular in our neighborhood: Twelfth and Oxford and Eighth and Diamond. We lived at 1922 N. Franklin Street, in the middle of the block, and almost every day those two gangs would come to the middle of our block and have a gang war. They used to shoot at one another; once I was hit in the leg by six pellets because I was outside when they started to fight. I fell and then jumped up screaming and ran into my house.

Often when these gangs came onto our block, we would go up on our roof with bricks. Twelfth and Oxford liked my brother and me, and we had friends in that gang: three members of the Hall family (Ronnie, Wilma, and Jolissie) and three boys from the Cooper family (Johnny, Frank, and William) that lived near Eighth and Montgomery. When Eighth and Diamond showed up, about ten of us threw bricks down at them. Every time we did, they searched all the abandoned houses looking for us. However, we knew every old house on that block and had many ways of escaping from them. To us, that was a good time. Many times I watched them fight and used to think it was fun.

On the days that the gangs were not fighting, I got together with my friends who lived close to my house: Landis, Brad, Little James, and Little Butch. We fought guys from the other end of the block, closer to Norris Street. We did exactly what we saw the big gangs doing. We'd throw rocks and bottles at one another. Together we would go to Tenth and Berks, where the government projects were, and fight the guys there.

Soon we started our own gang. Philip and his friend Brad were leaders. I became the leader of the little ones, and we called ourselves the Franklin Street Mambos. We also had Covance and his brothers Poopy and James. We would all get together and fight the Tenth Street Project gang, which included a guy named Bubbles. His gang said he was the toughest of all of them, and they wanted me to fight him.

On our way to fight Tenth Street Project, we saw Eighth and Diamond and Twelfth and Oxford running up Ninth Street like wild men. They started fighting right in the middle of the street, knifing each other. We backed up and ran down Eighth Street. This was supposed to be a free-for-all, where everybody could have a fair fistfight. Suddenly, the whole neighborhood was full of cops. As we sat back watching, it looked so exciting! I didn't realize that the more I saw of this violence and gang warfare the more curious I became and the more I desired to participate in it. After awhile, we started our own little gang and fought the kids up through the neighborhood. We were always in trouble.

Elementary School

I was in the fifth grade, going to school just around the corner from my house on Franklin and Norris, at Ferguson Elementary School. My teacher was a tall, heavy set black man named Mr. Brown. I was scared of him because he had a gigantic paddle. If you did something wrong, he would whip you with it. Most parents didn't complain about it; however, because they could not discipline their children themselves.

Other than a pair of twin girls named Martha and Myrna, I was the only Hispanic in the entire class. Everyone else was black, and many were the younger brothers of the Eighth and Diamond and Twelfth and Oxford gangs. I got into a number of fights with them because I wouldn't let them take advantage of me. I wasn't scared of anyone. If my father found out that I let people whip me and didn't do anything about it, he would whip me himself for my allowing them to beat me up. I was more afraid of my father than of other people. He always wore an angry look and constantly yelled at us. I was so afraid of him that I couldn't even look him in the face.

A new family moved into the neighborhood; there were six brothers and one sister named Mary. They got into a lot of trouble with us. After awhile, another Puerto Rican family moved into the neighborhood, with a daughter named Elizabeth and a son named John, who was very big for his age. There was also a girl in the neighborhood named Zuma. Zuma and Elizabeth used to have hooky parties at their houses while their parents were at work. Another girl, named Linda, lived next door to me and used to go to these parties. We would all hang out together, thinking we were having a ball as we got drunk. We would go to the liquor store and buy Thunderbird wine; we would go back, get drunk, and have sex. We would do this for about two weeks at a time, then go to school for a couple days, and then play hooky again. I remember Mr. Brown caught me after I had played hooky from his fifth grade class for about thirty days. I had stayed out sniffing glue and robbing people by breaking into their houses.

We had all kinds of parties at Elizabeth's house, and we would rob her brothers of their money. She would get into terrible trouble, but then we would do it again. Mr. Brown came to me one day and said, "Joey, you are a young man with a lot of potential in your life. You're bright. But I'm going to tell you something. The way you are going, you're not going to make it. You could end up like a lot of these young men, in prison for life or dead."

But I didn't listen to him. I never listened to anyone. I had my own agenda, my own plans about what I wanted to be in life and about what I wanted to do. And one of the

19

things I wanted to do was be a gangster because I already liked it. I realized that even though I was young — just ten years-old – I had a reputation. I would fight any kid on the block, and I could whip him. I was a good thief and almost always got away with it. Even though I was caught sometimes and locked up, I was perfecting my stealing.

When I was in the sixth grade, I missed almost three months of school. My father finally found out because the truant officers came to my house. I had missed so much school because I was hanging out at Elizabeth's house with Zuma and two other girls, Linda and Bertha. There were four girls and seven or eight boys. My brother Philip found out, and he started coming around with his friends. There were all kinds of wrong activities: drinking, promiscuous sex, and fighting. Some of the guys would get so drunk; they couldn't hold their liquor.

When my father found out what we had done, we were in big trouble. He punished us, whipping us so badly that he left marks on our bodies that lasted almost a month. He ripped the cord from the iron, folded it twice, and beat us so severely that he scarred us for life. It made me wonder if I really wanted to do those things again. But after awhile, things would cool down, and we would continue to steal and sniff glue.

We had every kid on the block – about ten or eleven kids – sniffing glue. We robbed people, smoked cigarettes, stole, and drank wine. Then we would go to other neighborhoods and break into houses. We broke into David and Matthew's house because we knew that David always had money. I remember one day when my friend Landis, from the Franklin Street Mambos, and I robbed David's house on Fourth and Berks Streets. We took about fifteen hundred dollars in cash and bought all kinds of things: drugs, glue, wine, and clothes. We bought silk and wool pants, EZ Walkers, double-knit shirts, and Converse sneakers, some of which we gave to our friends and families. If we weren't

20

locked up, we were getting in trouble.

My sixth-grade year was complicated by my teacher, Mrs. McAlly. She recognized the kind of trouble I was in and the path my life was taking. However, instead of trying to encourage me, as Mr. Brown had done, she constantly used me as a negative example in class. She would stand me up in front of the whole class and tell the other children that if I continued to go the way I was, I would be a nobody. She told them not to follow in my footsteps. I realize now that she acted out of concern for the others, but when she said these things, my heart hardened further. Of course, she was really upset with me for playing hooky from her class for three months. She was a beautiful black woman, but what she said hurt me so much that she broke my heart. There was always a battle in my mind between what Mr. Brown said about my potential and what Mrs. McAlly said about my never amounting to anything.

In 1968, my father decided to move back to Leithgow Street, but we only stayed there for a few months. I entered the seventh grade in the summer of 1968. I was eleven and supposed to go to John Wanamaker Junior High School, but I really didn't want to go there. I attended just a few times; then we moved back to Leithgow Street and my father had me transferred to Penn Treaty Junior High School. I had a good time there because my friend Joey was in the ninth grade, and I was in the seventh. Because Mikey had to repeat a grade, he was in the seventh grade with me. Joey's brother Bobby, my brother Philip, and my sister Evelyn were already in high school. Philip went to Edison High School for men, and Evelyn attended Kensington High School for women. Philip was always in trouble with the law and with my father. My father used to beat Philip all the time; he ended up in juvenile homes.

My father bought a bar on the corner of Third and Diamond. Then he decided to buy a house on the same block, and we moved to 2043 N. Third Street. We liked the neighborhood because it was full of young people who liked to party. There were a number of jitterbugs — gangsters — who hung out on the corner. There was a gang known as the Zulu Nation gang. They used to fight Eighth and Diamond, Marshall and York, the Mighties, and every now and then Twelfth and Oxford. There was a club of a few blacks and Hispanics called LSD — the Latin Soul Diplomats. They walked around the neighborhood wearing their jackets with the name of the club on them.

When we moved into that neighborhood, people had no idea who was moving in. It had been a nice area at one time, but after awhile, I think our neighbors wished we had never shown up. People already knew my father and my mother, and they recognized us because we used to go there to clean the bar. But now we were living right on the block. A guy named Sam and his deaf brother Jose lived next door to us. They had several sisters. Across the street lived a guy named Johnny. Down the street lived two Indian guys named Scott and Andy and two brothers, José and Junebug, whose father drove people to a farm to pick blueberries.

My brothers and I began to meet new people. Many of them were car thieves, and we got along well with them. After awhile, we created a new gang named Third and Diamond. Philip was the leader of the older guys, and I was the leader of the younger ones. I was about twelve-years-old then, in the seventh grade. My father bought a pool table to keep us out of trouble and put it in the basement. We would have the whole house full of guys — thirty to forty at a time. We drank, smoked cigarettes, sniffed glue, smoked marijuana, and took LSD. We would steal and then hide out in the basement of my house. Some of the guys were hustling to get money for our friends who needed bail because they were locked up for stealing cars. The majority of the guys hanging out in my basement were older — fifteen to eighteen-years-old — than I was. They liked to have me around them because I was a good thief like them.

Andy, Sam, Scott, José, and I would go downtown together every day. We would even play hooky from school just to go downtown and steal. Because my father owned a bar, I knew how to open cash registers; we went to Lit Brother's, John Wanamaker's, and Gimbels to steal the money from the registers there. Every single day we came home with three to four hundred dollars. We split it between four or five of us; I always had plenty of money. People liked to have me around.

There were times when I would go to the stores in Center City in downtown Philadelphia by myself, steal from the registers, and come home with three or four hundred dollars of my own. I would walk down the street and give my friends twenty dollars here, ten dollars there, fifteen dollars there. Philip would come and take $150 and then just smack me. I was so scared of Philip; he was the image of my father, always hitting me for no reason and pushing me around. Philip didn't want the younger boys to follow in his footsteps by doing the things we were doing. I also think he was jealous because I had the guts to do it, even though I was younger than he was.

After awhile, I started showing some of the kids in my neighborhood, who were twelve, thirteen, and fourteen-years-old, how to go downtown and steal. We would steal things we could sell. Often we were arrested by the police and ended up at the police station. From there we went to juvenile homes for two or three weeks at a time; no one knew where we were.

Chapter 3

The Runaway

By the age of twelve, I had already run away from home and started living in the streets. I heard one day that my father was angry and was looking for me because I wouldn't go to school. I had run away. Every now and then, I would sneak into the third floor of my house while my father was at work just to get a change of clothes. I would run across the roof, slip in the windows, and occasionally sleep under the beds. My mother used to cook extra food, put it in containers, put it behind our house, and whistle to let me know it was there.

Sometimes I would leave some money with my sister Debbie so that my brothers and sisters wouldn't tell my father anything. I gave her a little Flatsie Doll necklace, but she had to hide it so that my father wouldn't know she was seeing me. I would even give my brother Mikey as much as forty dollars at a time, but he would still tell my father any way. I remember during that time we found an old house on Third and Norris Streets. We cleaned it out, fixed it up, and put car seats in it to sit on; it was our own little house.

Meanwhile, my brother Philip ran away from home. Philip had spent time in a juvenile home for about eighteen months for stealing cars. He was considered the ringleader of a car theft group that had stolen thirty-two cars and kept them in our neighborhood. Philip, who was only fifteen or sixteen; my adopted brother Juan, whom we called Blueberry; and Billy were all in jail for car theft, weapons possession, and stealing other things. I was the only one left to stay with the gang.

When I ran away from home, several guys who used to hang around with my brothers also started running away from their homes. They came down to the neighborhood to hang out in the house I had cleaned and fixed up. During this time, there were always gang fights going on. Third and Diamond — my gang — was always starting trouble. We would go up to Third and Columbia Streets and have a gang war with the Puerto Ricans there. After awhile, the Zulu Nation considered us a part of their gang, and they called us the Low Lane Zulu. Many of their younger guys hung around us because they were aware that we knew how to steal, and we always had drugs.

Anything Not Nailed Down

We constantly broke into houses. Trucks would drive down the street with furniture in them, and we would start a big commotion on the corner of Third and Diamond to make it look as if there were a fight going on. While the truck driver was busy watching the fight, we would break into the back of his truck and take everything we could. We broke into the lamp factory at American and Diamond Streets and took lamps. Everyone on Third and Diamond and around our neighborhood got new furniture and lamps from what we had stolen. The people in the neighborhood didn't care. They were poor and didn't have money to spend on furniture.

Sometimes we would cause a cargo train to derail, and then we would take what we could sell. Consequently, the police were always patrolling our neighborhood; they hated us because we would get up on the roof and throw bricks down at them to bust their car windows. They called us the rock throwers. Every now and then we got arrested, and the police would take us down to the station and beat us up. When they found out we were from Third and Diamond, they really whipped us. They made us sit on the floor of our cells while they threw buckets of water mixed with lye onto us. Then they would open our cell doors, come in, and *walk on us.*

In fact, the whole district hated us because of the problems we created in our own neighborhood. We would have a gang war with the Irish and Polish kids on the other side of Second and Norris Streets. They used to call themselves P and D — Palethorp and Diamond. Once when we were fighting with them, I had a homemade double-barreled zip gun. Suddenly, one of them came too close to me. I ran toward him and unloaded both barrels. Two kids fell. The rest of their gang carried them back to their neighborhood. When everyone heard that I had shot two guys, it was a big deal. Naturally, I told everybody to keep quiet about it.

The Police Officer's House

Everyone we knew was getting arrested. We were taken to the police station and from there to juvenile homes. Finally, we were released into our parents' custody. However, because I was a runaway, no one knew where I was. I spent almost a month in the Youth Study Center before anyone in my family knew that I had been arrested. Eventually, I got out.

But as soon as I got out, I was arrested again. I knew two guys, Bobby and Darnel, from the Zulu Nation. They told me a police officer lived in our neighborhood. We decided to break into his house. At the time, I was waiting to go to trial for strong-armed robbery. But I broke into the officer's house anyway, stole his .38 and .22 pistols and three hundred dollars, and almost killed his father. The officer's father had seen my face, and I knew he could identify me. I was high from sniffing contact cement, and I tried to smother him with a pillow.

After I gave Darnel and Bobby some of the money, they fled. I had one gun on my right side and the other on my left under my T-shirt. I walked back to the policeman's

26

house, where there were cops outside and on the roof. As high as a kite, I went up to one of them and asked him what was going on. At that point, I didn't care if I was picked up or not because I was so miserable and lonely. I was living on the streets, sleeping in old cars and abandoned houses, and my father didn't want me at home. I went around to the back alley, where a fence had been knocked down. A neighbor and fellow gang member, José, lived there with his family. I took the gun with the holster and hid it under José's house.

At that time, José's neighbors, Papo and his wife, Martha, took me into their home and treated me like a son. They fed me and took care of me. Papo and Martha had three small children: Chino, Nancy, and Amy. I slept on the floor on blankets, and the family watched out for me. In return, I gave them money. Papo was like a big brother to me.

I told Papo I was the one who had broken into the police officer's house, and I had the gun, which I gave to him. But when I went back for the gun, I forgot to take the holster. Jose's sister Sonia saw me. She was one of the nosiest people in the neighborhood, and she told her father, who called the cops on me.

The next thing I knew, the police were looking for me. I had an open case for strong-armed robbery, and on top of that, I was in trouble for burglarizing a police officer's house and stealing his gun. I fled from the neighborhood for awhile.

At night I came back to hang out with the guys. They would go steal cars, and I was right there with them. I had no permanent place to stay. My sisters told me that my mother was crying at home at night because of me.

And I was miserable too. I remember one night I came to an old abandoned house. No one was outside; it was too cold. I pried up the tin that covered the windows to prevent people from getting into the house. I went inside and fell asleep, covering myself over with an old, dusty rug for warmth. The wind blew so strong that I was suddenly woken

27

up about three in the morning; I started to cry. I cried because I was so angry, so hurt, and so lonely. I wanted to go home, but my father would not let me come back. He had said that because I had left home, I could just stay away. That night the only thing I could think about was killing him.

Home Again

One day a black family moved to our neighborhood - an older lady we called Mrs. Mary, her son Dion, and a beautiful daughter named Sherry. I used to tell Sherry that she could be a model! She was about twenty-two-years-old and had a little daughter named Susie. Mrs. Mary found out I was living on the streets in an abandoned house. Many times she would see I was hungry and give me something to eat. Finally, one day she asked me to live with them. She gave me my own room and even my own television. Now I was living in the same neighborhood as my family, but I was living better than they were. Mrs. Mary loved me, and she really spoiled me.

After four months of being in the juvenile home, Philip was released. But when I got together with him, he was mean to me; he cursed at me and for no reason wanted to whip me. He was hanging out with the same bad crowd as before, and my father was upset because he wanted his children to have a different kind of life. So Philip ran away from home. The next thing I knew, he moved in with us over at Mrs. Mary's house. When Philip came to live there, he tried to control everything. He acted as if he were the boss of the house, treating Dion and me as if we were his slaves. Philip was just that type of person.

Meanwhile, I was still a fugitive. The cops were looking for me for burglarizing that police officer's house. One day, Sam's brother José (the one who was deaf) and I were sniffing glue in the Diamond Square Park on Howard

Street and Susquehanna Avenue. Suddenly, the police came up behind us and grabbed us both. They took me in and started questioning me about the gun that was stolen in the burglary. They wanted to find out what had happened to it. I never told them what happened. Instead, I told them I had never stolen a gun and didn't know what they were talking about. They beat me up to see if I would tell them about it, but I wouldn't say anything.

The cops put me in jail, and because I was a run away, no one knew where I was. I was held in the Youth Study Center for about a month until my father finally came and had me released. When he came for me, he yelled and cursed at me, threatening to beat me when we got home and to lock me up in a room for six months. I really didn't care if he did or not because I just wanted to be back with my family. When we arrived home, he didn't do anything to me. I was happy to be home again.

As I was waiting to go on trial for the burglary, Philip was again locked up, this time at the Philadelphia House of Correction. Around the same time, my father was also locked up in the House of Correction due to a riot with the police that had broken out in my neighborhood. My family was on the roof throwing bricks down at the cops while they entered our house by tearing down the door. They arrested Junebug and Johnny. My father fought with about ten police officers who were trying to subdue him. Although he was a short man, he was very strong, and I saw cops flying all over the place!

After awhile, the police were able to handcuff my father. They grabbed him by his long beard and dragged him out to the police wagon. My sister Evelyn came out of the house yelling at them, and then she started beating the cops; they beat her back, arrested her, and threw her in the wagon too. When the police snatched Junebug from under the bed, they didn't look again to see if someone else was under there. If they had looked again, they would have found me;

instead, I got away! All of this commotion made big headlines in the Philadelphia newspapers. After this incident, the cops were on the street corners constantly. This, of course, stopped the drug transactions for awhile.

The hangout for the drug addicts, drug dealers, and the Zulu Nation gang was Third and Diamond Streets. My father's bar was located on that corner and consequently was always full of members of both the Zulu Nation gang and the Third and Diamond gang. My father's cousin, Chencho cooked at the bar. It was a really busy community. There was always something happening on that corner; someone was getting shot or killed, or fights were breaking out between gangs. During this period, my brother Mikey and I were continually in trouble. We were locked up a couple of times together.

After a few days in jail following the riot, my father was back home. One day as we were sitting and watching television, a SWAT team broke into my house, knocking the door off its hinges. They ran through our house looking for my father, who was into the numbers racket. He also had a speakeasy because by law his bar couldn't be open on Sundays, and he was doing some racketeering in the streets. There were about twenty-five to thirty police officers with bulletproof vests looking for my father. For my brothers and sisters and me, this was big stuff! All the neighbors were watching the cops at my house with their riot helmets and equipment. This happened quite often to us. Many people in the neighborhood knew we were a family with big problems, and many of them didn't like us. Others, however, didn't care because they were involved in the same things we were.

A Chain Around My Neck

One day when I was about twelve-years-old, my father found out that I had been sniffing glue, and he was waiting for me to come home. I knew he was going to beat me, so I ran away. My adopted brother Blueberry had an old house where he was living, and I stayed with him. Just a few days later, as I was walking down the street, my father saw me. I ran from him, but he found me hiding in the basement of an abandoned house. He dragged me out of there and whipped me all the way home. When we got to the corner, he started bragging to his friends about what he was going to do to me. I was crying, trying to find a way to get away from him. He told his friends he was going to chain me up by my neck to make me an obedient son. His friends were laughing, but I hurt inside. I became angrier and angrier, and I started to hate his friends as well.

That day he took me home and chained me up by my neck in the basement for three days. Every day he came to the basement door and told me that he was going to make an obedient son out of me. My father drank, and the effects of alcohol caused him to lose his temper completely, acting irrationally. He didn't realize that while I was chained in the basement, instead of becoming the son he had hoped for, my heart was filling with bitterness and hatred.

I was able to convince my little sister Wandy to give me a butter knife to cut the chain, telling her that if she would get me the knife I would take her to my cousin Franky's house. I found out later that my older sister Gigi was beaten because Wandy had done this. It took me eight hours to cut through the chain. When I left the house, I took all the new clothes — two suitcases full – that I had bought with money from robbing the cash registers at Strawbridge and Clothier and John Wanamaker. Before I left the house, I wrapped a towel around my neck because I still had the padlock and chain on it.

I took my sister to Franky's house and went on about my business, walking to Blueberry's old house. When I got there, he was with some of his friends, and he asked what I was doing. He told me he had heard that my father chained

31

me up, and I told him it was true. When I took the towel off my neck, Blueberry and his friends saw the chain and started to laugh. We started sniffing glue while someone went to get a hacksaw to cut off the chain and padlock.

That day all I could think about was all the times my father had chained me up by my neck or feet or waist, and I imagined how I was going to kill him. I could still hear his friends laughing at me and mocking me as if it brought joy to their hearts. All the time I spent chained up; I promised myself I would murder my father. I didn't know that by thinking this way, I was opening my heart to evil and was allowing the spirits of darkness to take over my life. However, I could tell I was becoming angrier and more rebellious.

Three months later, I asked my mother if I could come home because the cops were looking for me. I still had to go to court for all the charges that remained open. I told her to ask my father if I could come home. When she asked him, he told her that I could come back but wouldn't be allowed outside the house. He locked me in my room for thirty days, putting a lock on the outside of that third-floor room. I spent every day locked up in my room. The only time I was allowed outside of it was to eat, and then I was put back in my room. However, although my parents thought I was locked inside the room, I knew how to get out. I would sneak out through the window in the middle of the night, do whatever I wanted to do, and then come back. After the thirty days were over, my father released me.

Chapter 4

Kicked Out of Philadelphia

It was 1969. I was waiting to go to court, facing three years in the juvenile home, and I was only twelve. But instead of going to court, I kept receiving preliminary hearings.

One day I got in major trouble again. I had gone with my neighbors Sam, Andy, and José to steal money from a cash register. Andy decided we should go to the Acme Supermarket at Adams Avenue and Roosevelt Boulevard. We walked in with a knife, demanded the cash register be opened, stole about $3,500, and ran. Because we weren't familiar with that neighborhood, we didn't realize a police station was just around the corner.

First, we ran into a school and went into the restroom to divide up the money. Then we went to a restaurant to get something to eat. This was at a time when sodas were ten cents; all we had on us were twenties and fifties. The manager of the restaurant was suspicious, of course, and called the police, although we weren't aware of it at the time.

We went outside, and a bus pulled up empty. The police must have cleared it. We got on, only to see a couple of cops, and ran right back off, only to realize the bus was completely surrounded by police. Squad cars squealed to a stop next to us. Only one of us got away. I was caught with about $1,500 on me.

The cops took us into the station, and they started to beat us. They wanted us to tell them where our friend who had gotten away lived. But I didn't know much about him. We had just moved into that neighborhood, and I didn't even know his real name. When they couldn't find him, they decided to send us to the Youth Study Center for a week.

When I walked into the center, everyone knew who I was because the supermarket stick-up was in all the newspapers, including *The Philadelphia Enquirer*, and in the television news. I was nicknamed Richie Rich after the cartoon character and referred to as the little rich boy due to my youth and the amount of money found on me. When I finally got out of the Youth Study Center, my father put me right back in that third-floor room again for another thirty days. He whipped me, but it didn't faze me. He could have hit me with a two-by-four, an extension cord, or anything else he wanted to use, but all of his beatings were to no avail. I didn't feel the pain; it was locked up in my heart as my anger and hatred toward him kept growing. After thirty days, he let me go again.

A Hardened Heart

I was now waiting to go to court for three new open cases against me, and I was still facing three years in the juvenile home, either at Glenmills or St. Gabriel Hall. I continued to be involved with the gangs, robbing people, and ripping old men's wallets out of their pockets. There was so much anger in my heart that I used to take little children to three-story buildings and hang them out the window. I told them, as they screamed and cried, that if they didn't rob their parents, I was going to drop them out the window and kill them. Because they were so scared, they stole from their parents and gave me the money so that I wouldn't hurt them. On two separate occasions, I threw one child off a third-floor roof and another from a second-floor window. One broke an arm, and the other broke both an arm and a leg.

My brother Mikey was filled with the same anger and hatred that I was. He used to yell back at my father, threatening to kill him. One day I told Mikey we were going to draft all the new guys in our neighborhood who weren't in gangs into ours. Mikey was thirteen and I was twelve. These new guys were fifteen and sixteen years old, but they were scared of us. They knew that we were violent and that we came from a very violent family. I had already stabbed and shot people. They knew that my father's cousin Chencho, who now had his own restaurant on Orianna and Diamond Streets, about a half block from my father's bar, had shot a man in the face, blowing his eye out. He had also been stabbed many times. My cousins were known to be people who would not hesitate to kill anyone.

We grabbed a group of these teenagers and lined them up in the street. I handed Mikey a dagger and told him to stand behind the last guy. We had seven guys in the line, all back to back. I told them that they had to pass a test to be part of my gang. Taking a shovel, I told them I was going to hit them three times. If anyone moved, the last guy in the line would be stabbed because Mikey was standing behind him with the dagger. I hit each of them three times, and not one of them dared to move. They were crying and in pain, but they didn't move. That's how they became part of us.

Many of the members in our gang had the same pain and anger in their heart as Mikey and I did. I remember Roberto, whom we called Coco, and his brother Rafael, whom we knew as Wino. Their father used to chain them up too. We also had Nelson, known as Black Boy. People from other neighborhoods heard about our reputation and wanted to be part of us. Many of them were junkies who wanted to be a part of the drug dealing in our neighborhood. We called our gang the Third and Diamond Young Boys; there were about sixty of us.

Sometimes when Zulu went out to fight other gangs, we would go with them to fight too. I grew up with many of the guys from the Zulu gang back on Franklin and Berks Streets. Covance was in Zulu, as were Poopy, Darnel, and many others. Many of them used to hang out in my father's bar, so they had a lot of respect for us, as well as for my father. Many of them feared my father and Chencho because they didn't take anything from anyone.

One day we went to fight a gang called Third and Columbia. As they began to shoot at us, Philip came out with an M-16 rifle, and Blueberry had a 30.30 Winchester. I don't know where they got them, but I knew they were stolen. There was a big shoot out, and later that same week Third and Columbia came back to fight us with another gang called the Anthill Mob. They numbered three hundred strong, and some of their guys were huge. That particular day our gang was dispersed all over the place. Only about five of us were on the scene at the time.

However, we stood our ground, and when Zulu heard what was happening, they came to help us. When the Anthill Mob saw them, they turned around and walked away. I remember the five of us were boxing these guys one at a time. They were hurting us, but we would not give up our ground. They had invaded our territory, and we had to keep it. Zulu gang had about a thousand members, but only three hundred of them showed up. Zulu could not believe we had stood our ground by ourselves, and that made them respect us even more.

Sent to Puerto Rico

At this point, I was continually in trouble and still waiting to go to court for all the open cases I had. When I finally went before the judge, I was twelve. I remember my mother crying in front of him. This not only embarrassed me, but when I saw her crying, I felt like getting up from where I was and stabbing her to death! I had only wanted my mother's love and concern, but I felt that I had to be labeled as a juvenile delinquent for her to weep over me. I was disgusted at what I saw as her hypocrisy.

My mother was crying on her knees before the judge, begging him not to put me away. She told him she would send me to relatives in Puerto Rico. I was so used to getting in and out of juvenile homes that in a way I was looking forward to going to jail.

However, the judge had sympathy for my mother and told her that I had to leave the city. She had one month to get rid of her thirteen-year-old son. I arrived in Puerto Rico on January 1, 1970. I remember how terrible I felt going to a place about which I knew nothing, and I started to cry. I didn't want to be there. I wanted to go home. To make matters worse, I thought everyone there was nothing but a hick.

That was also the first time I met many of my parents' relatives. My grandfather from my father's side was a tall, slender man who liked to shoot dice. My Aunt Maria was beautiful, and I loved her. She had an Indian complexion with dark black hair and lovely eyes. She was a real knock out; I noticed the way the men in the neighborhood were attracted to her. Aunt Maria had three children: two boys and one girl. She was separated from her husband, and men were always trying to get close to her. But she was also a very tough woman; she used to shoot dice too.

After being there a few weeks, I began to like Puerto Rico. It wasn't what I was used to, but I had no choice. My grandfather showed me how to shoot dice, teaching me a game called *Paripinta*. Every day when the newspaper vendor came by after selling all his papers, we would gamble. My grandfather gave me a few dollars so that I could play. There were many times when the vendor went home crying because we won all his money in the dice game! Sometimes my grandfather's friends came by, and I would shoot dice with them also. My Aunt Maria would stoop down just like a man to shoot dice. She also showed me a great deal of love, hugging me and treating me like one of her own children.

Back when I was in the United States, I had dropped out of eighth grade, which I had attended for only eight days. So when I went to Puerto Rico, I didn't go to school either.

After awhile, I met some of the neighborhood hicks. I started to show them guys – named Cheo, Eddie, and Felito — how to sniff glue. After doing that, we would go swimming in a little creek.

One day we went to a field where there were a lot of wild horses belonging to a man named Julio. For lack of anything better to do, we took one horse, tied him up by the legs, and hit him on the back. As he started to run, he tripped, breaking both of his front legs. We were in big trouble. When Julio told my Aunt Maria what had happened, she whipped me badly. I became so angry with her that all the anger I had in my heart toward my mother and father came to the surface; I wanted to kill her. One unforgettable trait about Aunt Maria was her discipline; she disciplined me differently than my parents did. After she hit me, the very next day she would hug me and tell me how much she loved me.

Philip was still getting into trouble back in the States. After my being in Puerto Rico for five months, my parents decided to send him there as well. I was so happy to see Philip that I didn't care if I had to stay there for another two years, as long as Philip was with me. We got along well with each other in Puerto Rico.

When my brother arrived in Puerto Rico, we began to do a number of things we shouldn't have done. We fought with all our cousins. My other grandparents owned a pig yard of about a thousand pigs, and they wanted Philip and me to clean it. However, every time we saw our grandfather coming, we ran and hid. We weren't about to clean a pigs' pen! We were city boys, not country boys. Because we didn't want to clean the pigs' pen, we wouldn't even visit our mother's father because he always had that special job for us.

Sometimes we went onto private property and rode other people's horses. Once, someone gave me a female horse to ride that was pregnant. We took her to the field to ride her, but as we were crossing a creek, she slipped and broke her legs. She was so badly hurt that she died. We dug a hole four feet deep and eight feet square. We put tires, dry leaves, and grass on the carcass to burn it. We were in terrible trouble for that!

One day as the ice-cream man was coming down the street, Philip, Cheo, Felito, my cousin Johnny, and I took some rubber bands and used u-nails, the type used to hold down wires, to shoot at him. Philip, however, shot the man in his eye and almost destroyed it. My Uncle Lolo, who had just moved back to Puerto Rico from the States, whipped us so badly that we didn't want to stay in Puerto Rico any more. In my anger, I wanted to kill him too. All of us were punished, and the next thing we knew, my grandmother called my father to tell him she was going to send Philip back to the United States.

I was so disappointed that I told them I would kill myself if they sent Philip back without me. My parents had no other choice but to send for both of us. I had been in Puerto Rico for only six months and seventeen days.

Chapter 5

Into Worse Trouble

According to the courts, I was not allowed back in the States for eighteen months. I had to be careful not to get caught. As soon as I got back, everybody was happy — all my friends, my brother Mikey, and my sisters. I noticed that many new people had moved into the neighborhood; some of the new guys were not treating my sisters with respect. My sisters described how they were being treated. Within a few days, I was whipping guys left and right, robbing them, and taking their money. Their parents already hated me, calling me a child of the devil and saying that the demon had come back. No one wanted me around because their children became more vicious and violent under my influence.

Philip started hanging out with his old friends again and ended up shacking up with a girl named Maria. I felt sorry for her because Philip used to treat her as if she were a dog. He hit her and practically tortured her. Once he hit her with a golf club, yet through all that she still stayed with him. At the time I thought she must have really loved him to stay with him under those conditions.

I wasn't home long before I started getting in trouble again. My brother and I were still drafting new kids into our gang. Another gang called the Homiciders existed in our neighborhood. Louie Burgos, Papo's younger brother, ran that gang. They were really like another part of our gang; we would help each other whenever it was needed.

By this time, many teenagers were sniffing glue and other substances. We got into selling a liquid called Tiewal Paint Thinner. We found the factories that made it, and we broke in to steal it. Sometimes we stole fifty-five-gallon drums. We could sell a soda bottle full of it for five dollars. Tiewal Paint Thinner became a big moneymaker. The junkies liked what we were doing and respected us. Even the guys on the corner respected us because they knew we didn't play games. We weren't scared of anyone.

Back home there was still more trouble. My sister Evelyn left home and ran away with her boyfriend, John. My father was looking for John to kill him. After awhile, Philip also moved on. He and Maria had broken up, and he started living with another woman, Mae. I felt it was the best thing for Maria. Near the end of 1972, much was going on. We were still causing trouble, gang warring with every one we could find and stabbing and shooting people. We just didn't care anymore. Our gang became even more violent.

Zulu

One day the Zulu Nation gang allowed my *walky* (a guy you hang out or walk around with), Little Midnight, and me to drink and get high with them; they respected us because they knew we wouldn't hesitate to kill anyone. My friend Larry (called Bird) and James (Covance's brother), who used to live on Franklin Street, also joined us in the drinking. Midnight and I were the only Puerto Ricans in that gang, and we had to box twenty guys just to get in. I wanted to get in Zulu because there were two or three guys already in it with whom I wanted to get even.

To get *out* of the Zulu Gang, a guy had to box about *fifty* guys. Many times a person wanting to leave didn't make it out alive. If he was alive by the time the gang finished beating him up, it was because God had mercy on him!

We also had another way, called Kangaroo, of getting out of our gang. My brother Mikey was the kangaroo judge of the Third and Diamond gang. We would line up the guys from the gang and join hands. The one who wanted out would have to run straight through that barrier. We would tell the guy who wanted out how many times he had to run through. Some guys who ran made it only two or three times.

41

Others made it only once. By the time he had done it, he might have been stabbed or received a broken head and broken bones.

The Zulu gang had the same rituals. They would box us, but we stood strong all the way to the end. I knew a number of the Zulu members because many of them used to hang out in my father's bar. They always treated me as if I were one of them, and finally I became a member of their gang. Our leader's name was Cat. We had about 150 young boys in this division of the Zulu gang, which consisted of six divisions.

On one occasion, Zulu had to go to the funeral of Big Bogard, one of the old heads, or older guys, who had just been killed in a car accident. On our way back home we had to pass through Eighth and Diamond Streets, which was an enemy gang's territory. However, because the cops knew we had to go through that location and knew we were rivals, they decided that nine police cars would escort us to and from the funeral. The police didn't want to leave us alone because they knew our reputation for starting trouble. There were so many of us walking down the street that we covered ten long city blocks on both sides.

Police were on every corner, and detectives were all over the place. Zulu had a reputation for being one of the largest and most violent gangs in North Philadelphia. The old heads spent their time drinking wine and getting high. They all liked me even though I was Puerto Rican. They knew I was crazy and would shoot or stab anyone. Sometimes they would give me the gun to do the shooting because I was underage. Other times they wanted me to trip and knock down someone. Nobody expected a Hispanic to be part of the Zulu gang.

Members of the Zulu gang in 1972

The Break Up of Our Family

My parents were having worse problems than ever. I was never around their neighborhood anymore. When I became a member of the Zulu gang, I hung around with the gang members all the time. After awhile, my parents separated. My mother and father never were married to each other although they had lived together for many years and produced ten children. My father was messing around with another woman, and my mother wanted to show him that she could live the same way. She began to live with another man, not knowing how much more this would cause her to suffer. She rented a house in the 4500 block of Mole Street, near Mole and Wingohocking Streets. My father stayed in the other house. His girlfriend was about fifteen years younger than he was, and I lived with them for awhile. However, I hated his girlfriend and treated her like a dog. After a few months, they found another place to live.

He left the house to my older sister Evelyn, who was also watching over us. Philip was in jail at the time. An Irish woman named Sharon and her Hispanic girlfriend, Doris, also took care of us. They moved in with us for about a month; even though I was old enough to take care of myself, my younger brothers and sisters weren't.

All kinds of people were coming and going from that house, and all kinds of things were going on. My brothers and sisters fought continually, and we did whatever we wanted because there was no one to tell us what to do. When my mother found another place to live, she took my younger brother and sister, Willie and Wandy, to live with her. The rest of us stayed behind because we didn't like the man with whom she was living.

We stayed at the house on Third and Diamond, still doing the same crazy things — sniffing glue, stealing, gang warring, and breaking into factories and people's houses. We tried to get money any way we could. I remember being so angry, so frustrated, and so miserable at that time. I was only fifteen when my parents split up in 1972.

One day I told my gang that I was going to kill someone. They looked at me as if I were crazy. Every time we went out, I tried to kill someone just to take my frustration out on society. On one occasion, some members of the Sixteenth and Wallace Streets gang came to visit us. They were what we called a neighbor gang because they joined with us to get high. They decided to go to Marshall and York Streets or Eighth and Diamond neighborhood to hurt someone. It was already in my heart anyway, so we all agreed.

We started walking toward those neighborhoods; some of us had guns, and others had knives. As we walked down the street, we ran into some young guys who belonged to another gang. We ran up on them and started to beat them up. They fell down but got away staggering.

Two days later, the arrests began. The cops arrested the whole gang. I was already on probation and had another attempted murder pinned on me for which I was going to court. Now I was being investigated along with thirty other teenagers. However, the police released me because they said I wasn't from the Zulu gang.

I wasn't out for too long because my probation officer caught up with me the next day. I was almost sixteen and facing close to five years in prison. I was in so much trouble that the courts wanted to give me every sentence they could pin on me just to get me off the streets.

But the police had to release me because they couldn't find any evidence for the charges that they had against me. When I went before the judge, there was talk of giving me a three to five-year sentence. However, my lawyer, my probation officer, and the judge agreed that instead of prison I would be sent to a government program. If I finished two years with good behavior, I didn't have to do the third year.

Indiana

I was sent to the Attabury Job Corps, a government program in Indiana about a half-hour from Indianapolis. I remember getting ready to go. Everyone was happy for me, and I was happy also because I was already becoming too violent and wanted to get away from that environment. There was no peace in my life, and I wanted to change. My mother finally took the rest of my siblings to live with her. Evelyn and Philip were already on their own, and I was being sent to a government program to do my time.

My gang buddies collected liquor and drugs, and we were all drinking and getting high. They were laughing and making jokes about my coming back soon, telling me that I never stayed long anywhere. But I told them I wasn't coming back at all. And if I *did* come back, I was going to be a totally different man. I was changing my life. I kept remembering what Mr. Brown said back in fifth grade when he told me I had potential.

That day I got so high that I could hardly get up the next morning to leave for the government program. Finally, I managed to pack my clothes, and I departed. I didn't say good-bye to anyone, not even to my family. I just left. I got on the Amtrak, which took about twenty-four hours to reach Indianapolis. During my trip, all I could think about was changing my life. Everyone had told me I could get my GED (General Equivalency Degree) in this program or learn a trade and come out able to get a good job. I thought the Job Corps was going to be a paradise, not realizing it was actually going to be another hell. I didn't know the same train was transporting about twenty guys from Philadelphia, about sixteen from New York, and a few from Baltimore and Washington, DC.

When I arrived, a bus came to pick me up. As it drew closer, I realized I wasn't the only one to be picked up. Approaching the center, I saw a group of guys waiting out side. There were many buildings, some yellow and some blue. The yellow buildings were the honor dorms, and the blue buildings were the ghetto dorms. Around another building, guys were dressed in army fatigues with nametags. It looked to me like a concentration camp. I had absolutely no idea what I was getting into.

Finally leaving the bus, we were taken to a room and given numbers. My number was 0323019, which meant I had arrived in the third month and the second week of 1973, and I was the nineteenth person to arrive that day. About a hundred or more guys were in the orientation room. A tall, tough-looking black man came into the room and introduced himself as Mr. Ship. At first, I thought he was a religious man because he told us to bow our heads in prayer before he started the orientation. So we all bowed our heads and supposedly prayed with him; I certainly didn't know anything about prayer and looked at him as if he were crazy.

After he finished praying, he started cursing

everything in sight. He practically cursed the paint off the ceiling. As he did so, he put fear into our hearts. He let us know he was not playing games with us. He had me completely in left field somewhere, and I thought, "What have I gotten myself into now?"

Chapter 6

The Job Corps

Right after orientation, we were taken to where we would sleep and were assigned a bed. We would be in this building for two weeks in a vocational orientation. After that, we would be assigned to our dormitories. Next, they took us outside to the barber, who scalped everyone down to a baldhead. I never had a baldhead before in my life. I was only sixteen and had no idea what was going on. I didn't know where I was.

Later we were taken to another room, where we had to sit for quite some time. As I sat there, I remember what Lefty had told me about these government programs. Lefty was in our gang and had just come home from the same government program himself. He said that at the government programs it wasn't corner fighting corner. When you got there, *all* the gangs from Philadelphia stayed together. Back home, they would kill each other, but in the program they all pulled together and hurt anyone from the other cities or states. He had told me that Philadelphia and New York would fight Chicago and Detroit. His advice was to just hang with the guys from Philadelphia.

While I was sitting there, a couple of guys asked if there was anyone from Philly. So I with my big mouth said, "Yeah, I'm from Philly! What's the matter? You don't like it?" I thought the guys wanted to fight, and I was ready to fight back.

They, however, backed off and said, "Calm down! What's your problem? We're from Philly too." They asked me what gang I was from, and I told them I was from Zulu. A couple guys from two other gangs were with me. Another guy there decided to go to the Job Corps on his own because he wanted to do something for himself. When I told them I was from the Zulu gang, they nicknamed me Zulu. They went to get a guy named Little Easy, who was from the same gang in Philly. He came to see me and gave me his own orientation about what to expect.

I discovered that about 2,300 teenagers comprised the program. The majority of them had been sent by a judge, but some had come on their own. Little Easy told me, "Here we're fighting Chicago, known as "Chi-Town." Philadelphia was known as "Phillythang." He also told me not to worry because Philadelphia had a powerful reputation there. One of the guys who came with me from Philly, a tall, thin black brother named Kenneth, whose nickname was Smiley, became walkies with me. He was from the Tenderlines at Thirty-first and Huntingdon. We were always hanging out together and went through the orientation together. But once we were assigned to our dorm, we were split up.

Third and Diamond and the Homiciders gang in 1972

A Leader

While we were in orientation, we realized it wasn't going to be an easy place. I already realized it wasn't the paradise I had imagined. Smiley was sent to dorm 1011, and I was sent to dorm 1010. When I walked into the dorm bay area, I saw twelve beds. All the orientation guys had to sleep in the same room. I remember our dorm manager, Mr. O'Neill, a black man with a good attitude. Mr. O'Neill looked at me and made me the bay leader. This meant I was responsible for making sure the twelve guys always kept the room clean and followed the rules every day.

The dorm wings had a total of thirty-eight guys in them; twelve slept in the bay, and the rest slept in their own rooms, which had showers. After proving yourself worthy of the private rooms, you would be transferred to them. I was just happy being the bay leader. I started meeting guys from all over the United States, and I was responsible for providing them with all the cleaning supplies needed to keep the rooms spotless.

Mr. O'Neill liked me a lot, and I was trying to work hard to be a good bay leader because I wanted to go to a room in the wings. In the bay, people would break into your locker and steal your money and possessions. But in the wing, you would have your own room and your own shower. You didn't have to take a shower with two or three other guys. A roommate was assigned to you, but it was much better than sharing a room with eleven other people.

After thirty days Mr. O'Neill assigned me to a room and made me the wing leader. Now I was in charge of thirty-eight guys in this wing. My assistant wing leader was Rodney from New York, and Gary was my bay leader. He had an assistant bay leader under him. Every month we had to do GI, which consisted of stripping the whole floor and cleaning it completely. I showed them what to do, and they would do it. While they were cleaning the floor, I would go around to visit all the guys from Philly. I found out there were 450 young men there from Philly, and I started hanging out with them. I got high only every now and then because there were no drugs in the center unless somebody smuggled them in. Sometimes a few guys would manage to sneak in some wine; just the smell of it got us high because our systems were cleaned out from being in the center.

Trouble

After awhile, Mr. O'Neill quit his job and was replaced by a man named Mr. Dixon. This man looked as if he didn't like anyone! Every time he told me to do some thing, I did it. However, I was already creating trouble. Smiley and I had become good friends, and we started trouble together. Even though there were about 450 guys from Philly and even though we weren't back home gang warring, sometimes we would just free-for-all with each other. The yellow dorm would free-for-all with the blue dorm.

Every now and then we would get into serious trouble with the guys from Chicago. Sometimes we would find ourselves in the movie theater, and someone from Chicago would throw an A battery over to our side of the chairs. In return we would throw batteries back. The security guards would have to try to stop a fight that had broken out. As many as ten security guards with black jacks in their hands were ready to club people upside the head. At times, they stopped us from going to the movies at all because of the fights that would break out in there with Philadelphia and Chicago.

Smiley and I enjoyed quite a reputation in this government program. We wrote graffiti on the walls; I would write down the name of my gang, Zulu, and Smiley would write his name. About five months later, a reward of fifty

51

dollars was put out to find Zulu and Smiley.

We also cut class and went to the old German graveyard. At one time, before this had been a center, it was a prisoner-of-war camp for captured German soldiers during World War II. Often we would break into the old buildings that had never been fixed up for the center. Sometimes we found bombs and hand grenades in there, but they didn't have gunpowder in them. We brought them back with us, and every time we would have a free-for-all, we would use those grenades as a joke, throwing them at the guys.

Attabury Job Corp in 1973

Each month we received thirty dollars for being in the program, and we used it for gambling. Sometimes, however, I would go to the snack bar and use my money to buy candy or pies to resell for double the price. If people wanted credit, they would have to pay four times what the item was worth. These guys would pay it! I was making a good hustle, selling all of these snacks in my closet. If I had been caught,

I would have been penalized for it and would have had to pay a fine. But I was never caught. When we shot dice, sometimes I lost all my money. Other times I would beat the others out of their money.

After being in the center for about eight months, I received a pass to go home. I was really looking forward to it because I was homesick. I had continued to write letters to Mikey, Vivian, and their friends, and now I wanted to go home to visit them. I was given a fourteen-day pass, but I ended up taking twenty-seven days instead.

When I got to Philly, I threw a big party and got high again. I got extremely drunk the day I got home. It was the end of September 1973. I started going out with Zulu again, and it seemed that I had become even wilder and more violent in the government program. I ran up to a gang on Eighth and Diamond Streets to shoot someone before going back to the center.

On one occasion, some guys from Eighth and Diamond came around the liquor store on Germantown Avenue and Norris Street. There were three of them and four of us, so we started to chase them. This was a trap because as we came around the corner, there was a guy waiting for us with a shotgun. I was ahead of my guys, and as I drew close to the guys we were chasing, one jumped out of the alley and pumped the shotgun. But it jammed. When I saw that, I grabbed the shotgun and hit him with it. He started to run, and I dropped the shotgun and raced after him. But just as quickly, we decided to let him go. We turned around and went back to the liquor store. Things like this were constantly happening to me. I faced death so many times, but I didn't care if I died. I hated myself anyway and everyone else too. I didn't care if I was shot or even killed. Many times I wanted to die because I hated my life.

I was supposed to go back to the government program on October 1973, but Zulu was planning to gang war that night. I told them, "Since I'm leaving, give me the gun. I want to do the shooting." They gave me a .38. I went with four guys from Zulu — Kimba, Barry, Little Kimba, and Baron — around the back of Dolphin Street. Meanwhile, Mikey, my brother Edwin, Pewee, the rest of the guys from Third and Diamond, and the guys from Zulu were coming west on Susquehanna Avenue. Five of us went to the back to help them trap our enemies.

We came around Ninth Street and Dolphin and then went down Ninth Street to Susquehanna. When we got there, a lot of guys from Eighth and Diamond were hanging out on the corner. Seeing them, we started running toward Seventh Street because the rest of our guys were coming up Susquehanna Avenue. Someone yelled out, "Zulu is behind you!" As they turned around, I just began to shoot. My gun jammed up at first, but then it started firing. A couple of guys fell, and when I looked up, I saw another one hiding behind a car. I put the gun to his head to blow him away. He started screaming, but when I tried to fire, the gun jammed twice. I just let him run away.

I passed all the others and arrived at Fourth and Susquehanna. I threw the gun into an abandoned house and waited for the rest to show up. All of a sudden, cops were all over the place. That night I went home as if nothing had happened.

The following day I got on the bus and went back to Indianapolis. Mikey wrote me about a month later to tell me that no one died in that shooting. However, the Eighth and Diamond Street gang was now looking for the one who did the shooting. When I arrived back at the program, I told the others some of the things I had done while I was home. I wanted to return to Philadelphia, but I knew I couldn't. I had to stay longer in Indiana because I was sentenced to the program.

Education

   While I was in the program, I took body and fender classes. I figured that maybe some day I could open a body and fender shop of my own. However, I didn't really like it too much. I tried everything. Arriving at the program, I was at the three hundred level in reading; I could hardly read or write. But while I was studying there, I brought my reading up to the nine hundred level, which was equivalent to the ninth grade. I was on my way to the twelve hundred level, where I could take a test to get my G.E.D. I found myself really striving for this because I wanted to have my G.E.D. I also wanted to finish with some kind of trade so that I could do something with my life. I graduated from body and fender in nine months. Because I still had the remainder of my sentence to carry out, I took a cooking course. I thought that perhaps some day I could open my own restaurant. Once we even cooked for the governor of Indiana and for the mayor of Indianapolis. That was important to us!

   After a few months, I was transferred to another dormitory, an honor dorm. It was dorm 1003, one of the cleanest in the entire program. I was made dorm president. Even though I was in trouble a lot, I remember thinking that someone must be on my side because all the dorm managers liked me.

   As the dorm president, I had six wings to oversee, with a total of 156 guys. Six wing leaders and six assistant wing leaders helped me. All the rooms in 1003 had two beds, and every room had its own shower. I took good care of that dorm. We always won awards and were complimented for being one of the cleanest dorms in the entire program.

Attabury Job Corp in 1973

However, our ways didn't change. After school, we would sneak into town on the weekends. Some guys would smuggle in some marijuana, and we would get high on it. Sometimes we wanted to get high so badly that we would sniff gasoline, paint, or paint thinner — anything that would get us high — if there were no drugs or alcohol.

We had a night manager whom I liked to hear talk because he had a real southern accent. His name was Mr. Brewer, and he always wore his cowboy boots and his big cowboy hat. One day he said to me, "You got KP today, Zulu." Everyone, even the dorm managers, called me Zulu. He said, "I want you to push the kitchen line today." I had to rotate twenty-four guys during breakfast, lunch, and dinner for a whole week. Once a month, our dorm had to do KP, and every day these twenty-four guys would feed over two thousand in the center. Mr. Brewer always got good reports about the job we were doing and complimented us because we were doing so well.

But this time, when my dorm had KP, I was headed for some of the worst trouble of my life.

Chapter 7

Return to Philly

While I was doing this KP, a guy from Chicago walked up to me and asked me if my name was Zulu. I said yes. He also asked me if I was from Philadelphia, and I said I was. Then he said that later on that night in the theater Philly and Chi-town were going to "have it out." When he said that to me, I looked back at him and told him that we would be ready.

As the guys from Philly began to come through the line, I started telling some of them what was going on. At the same time, I was stealing butter knives and dicing knives and passing them on to our guys as they came by with their trays. When we went to the movies that night, we were planning to do some "heavy duty hurting." But once we got there, nothing happened.

Two days later, however, all the trouble started. We went to a few of the dormitories, where we found a couple of guys from Chicago and Detroit. We got right in their faces and started fighting them. We threw some of them off second-floor balconies, and we took others out the back way and threw them down the steps. Soon what had begun as a fight escalated into a riot. The security guards were brought over to stop it, and some of our guys turned over security cars. The security guards called the army base across the street because there were too many of us. Finally, they restored peace to the program.

"No Evidence"

After everything settled down, about forty guys from the program were injured, six security guards were wounded, and three cars were turned over. The next day, local and federal officers and soldiers from across the street arrived. They started an investigation, going from dormitory to dormitory trying to find out who had started the riot. About a week later, they came to get me and took me to a security office. Federal investigators were there, and they started asking me questions and smacked me around a few times.

I remember that when I first walked in, Captain White, a security guard, picked me up by my shirt collar, lifted me off the ground, looked in my face, and asked, "Is your name Zulu?" When I told him yes, he laughed and asked, "How in the world did you get a name like Zulu? The Zulu are a black tribe in Africa." Then he threw me down. He looked at me again and repeated, "How did you get the name Zulu?" I told him I was from Philadelphia and belonged to a gang called the Zulu Nation.

When I said that, everyone in the room laughed because I had light skin, curly hair, and I didn't look black. They took me to another room, and a few other guys came in and had a little party smacking me around. They told me they were going to throw me out of the program.

They had this young guy named Blake from Washington, DC. His testimony was the only evidence they had against me. Blake had been in the cafeteria line and had heard the guy from Chicago tell me what was going to happen in the movies that night. They asked him if he would testify against me in court, and he agreed. So they let him go that day while I stayed locked up for another three days. The federal investigators told me I was going to prison, and from there I would be sent to a federal penitentiary. I was not quite seventeen-years-old at the time.

I really didn't care what they did to me. But the first thing that ran through my mind when I sat in the cell for three days was that I wasn't going to see my family for a long time. When it was time to go to court, Blake never showed up. The guys from Philly had threatened to kill his whole family back home if he testified. They told him they were going to send people from Philadelphia to Washington, which was only three hours away, to kill them. He became so scared that he told the federal officers he didn't know who the guy was who had started the riot. Because they no longer had a witness, they had to drop all the charges.

Impossible to Change

Even though I thought about changing my life, it was too difficult for me to do. I couldn't figure out why I kept looking for trouble. After I did my time in the government program, I went back to Philadelphia.

After being home for three months, I received my readjustment check from the Job Corps for seven hundred dollars. I promised everyone I would buy wine the day my check came. I bought a case of wine for the old heads from Zulu and another case for the guys I was hanging out with on American and Allegheny Avenues, younger guys from Zulu and Third and Diamond. I also bought everybody hamburgers.

We became so drunk that when some teenagers came out of school, we stopped them and asked them what gang they were from. One kid got smart with me and threw a punch. Before he could hit me, I knocked him down with my stick, a bamboo cane, and popped him upside his head twice. Then I hit him a third time with the cane, breaking his arm. He started to run, so we chased him.

The next thing I knew, I was telling the cops what had happened. They locked me up for aggravated assault. A friend of mine who had also been in the Job Corps with me, Hardrock from the Morocco gang, was drinking with me that day. When he came back from chasing the other guys, he too was arrested. I was sent to the Youth Study Center because I was just seventeen-years-old. Because Hardrock was nineteen-years-old, he was sent to the Philadelphia Detention Center. About a week later, I was out again. As soon as I got out, I went back to getting high with my friends. But now I had new charges against me.

Sometime later we went to war with an enemy gang, Fifth and Westmoreland. They had stabbed one of the guys from Fourth and Huntingdon, a guy whom we called Little Man. When we found out that he had been stabbed, we went looking for the guy who did it. Upon finding him, he began chasing us with a jack. We all jumped over a fence, but his pants got caught and he fell.

I saw this, went back, and hit him upside his head twice with a stick. Then I grabbed him by the neck and stabbed him four times with a screwdriver. After I dropped him, he jumped up and started to run home. He kept on falling to the ground but would get back up and run until he made it home. After that, a group came around our neighborhood looking for us on Indiana Street. They knew whoever had stabbed that guy hung around Fifth and Indiana. When we realized they were looking for us, we started to arm ourselves with guns.

Philip's brothers-in-law, Rafael and Manny, had a .32 pistol, and they gave it to me. Smiley had a sawed-off .22 rifle. When these guys found out we were strapped down with weapons, they never came back looking for us.

We continued to build our reputation in the neighborhood. We kept hanging around Fourth and Indiana Streets, a few blocks away from my father's house. Because I was living with him again and many of the guys I was hanging with — Richie, Lemon, and Gun — lived in that neighborhood, it was easier for all of us to be together. We drank and got high every day and warred with other gangs.

Midtown Zulu

Even though Zulu was one big gang, it was split into many divisions, which joined together when going to fight different gangs. One day when we were all high, we started talking about making one big gang of our own. I hadn't been down to the Zulu gang neighborhood for about a month, and to walk out of Zulu was not easy. To be a member, you had to be with them at least four days out of the week. So Larry, Black Hook, Baron, and Soul, the leader of the young boys, came to Indiana looking for me. But they didn't want to start any trouble.

I had become tired of hanging out with them, and I didn't want to be around them anymore. I wanted to be on my own. I figured since I returned so wild from the Job Corps, I would start my own gang. Soul and Hook asked me, "Why don't you start Midtown Zulu in this neighborhood? Everyone who was from it before is either dead or in jail. There is no more Midtown Zulu up here. You should start it back up. That way you don't have to go through the line to get out." It was a good idea, so we all joined together: Mikey, Lemon, Peewee, Gun, Richie, and even some of the guys from Fourth and Indiana. Midtown Zulu wasn't just a black gang. It was mixed, the majority being Hispanic.

There were about sixty of us. But we didn't stop there; we started to draft every small gang we found in the neighborhood. We started on Franklin and Indiana, and by the time we finished, we had about 250 in our gang. Soon other guys heard about our reputation, and they joined us as well. Every time we went to parties, people would pay us *not* to come in. But after we took their money, we went in anyway and turned that party upside down.

Whenever we went to the movies, we would start a fight with other gangs. No one liked us. We would even fight with the old heads. Although we were only seventeen to nineteen-year-olds, we would fight men much older than we were. We were crazy. People would shoot at us, trying to kill us, and we would shoot back at them. We would blow up their cars. If people moved out of the neighborhood and planned to sell their house, by the time they came back, they didn't *have* a house. We would break all the windows, rip

61

out the doors, and sell the copper pipes. We did anything we could to obtain money to buy wine and drugs to get high.

Members of the Zulu gang in 1973

There were some homosexuals who lived in our neighborhood, and we discussed moving them out. Instead, we talked to one of them named Val and told him that if they wanted to keep living in the neighborhood, they would have to pay us protection dues. They agreed. Val used to give me guns as his dues so that we wouldn't do anything to him or the drag queens. Even though we were violent, many people in our own community liked us because we protected them. If somebody walked into our neighborhood trying to start some kind of trouble with anyone of them, we would side with our neighbors, even if they were in the wrong, and we would "put a hurting" on the other people. Once they left, they never came back.

A Change Within

As the days passed, I grew more and more quiet. I became the first leader of the gang, and Richie was the second leader. Mikey was the kangaroo judge, and Lemon was the warlord. We continued to war with other gangs and get high. We would go to Fifth and Allegheny to the Recreation Center and get drunk with the Uptown Zulu gang. Sometimes we would go to Diamond Street and get drunk with the Downtown Zulu gang. If they were fighting somebody that day, we would fight with them. Many of our guys got locked up for stabbing and shooting people. Smiley was locked up because he was caught with a .22 sawed-off rifle, and he was facing three years. Instead of going to jail, he enlisted in the army before he could be sentenced and ended up going to Germany.

A few months later, I was arrested with a .32 pistol. I almost blew a teenager's brains out on Fifth and Westmoreland Streets. I didn't shoot him because a woman kneeled before me and begged me not to kill him as I held the gun to his neck. I felt sorry for her and let him go. She and everybody else in that neighborhood knew I would have killed him, but for some reason that I couldn't explain, I didn't.

However, they called the police, and I was caught with the gun and arrested for it. I ended up again in the Juvenile Center for about three weeks. When I came out, I had a gun charge against me and an aggravated assault charge. All of the young men in my gang feared me. Some were punks and cowards, but by the time I was finished with them, they had a heart to fight and kill anyone and die for me. Some of them dared to jump in front of guns and rifles. People shot at us, and instead of running away, we ran toward them.

I would wake up in the middle of the night lonely and miserable. I would have terrible nightmares of people killing me. My stabbing and shooting so many people haunted me wherever I went. I felt that someday I would die a horrible death. But of course, I could not show how I was feeling inside to my friends; they looked at me as a god. They thought I was the greatest person in the world. Even the young girls in the neighborhood looked up to me. When I went to parties, I didn't have to ask any girl to dance. They would come and *ask* me to dance with them. Some of them just wanted to be my girlfriend because of the reputation I had. Many of them felt that by being my girlfriend they could start any trouble they wanted, and people would leave them alone. I tried to stay away from trouble, but it wasn't working.

I remember that one day about seventy of us were gang warring on Westmoreland Street. There was another gang throwing bricks at us, and we were throwing some back at them. Suddenly, two guys jumped off the steps. One of them had a rifle, and the other had a .38 handgun. All I had was a mop stick, but I ran toward them yelling, "Kill me! Kill me! *You don't have the heart to kill me!*" When I finally got close to them, I realized they had frozen in their tracks. They turned around to run into the house, but Mikey and the others were right behind me; we ran in after them. We beat them with the mop sticks and even hit their parents. As we ran out the door, the cops were running in, and we told them that there were some people in there trying to kill someone. The cops didn't know it was us, so we got away that day.

Chapter 8

Close Encounters with Death

I had just bought two gallons of wine. We all got drunk. We were with Rafael, one of the guys from our gang. He owned a Chevy Nova, and we decided to go back to our neighborhood. Three guys were in the front seat, and four of us rode in the back when the car broke down on Orianna and Lehigh Streets across from Church's Chicken. As we tried to push the car, some black guys came out of a house and started arguing with us. One guy argued with Rafael because he wanted the car off the pavement. We were attempting to do just that, but he continued to argue.

A big fistfight broke out. One of the guys punched Rafael. We were outnumbered ten to seven. We threw bricks at them and hit them with sticks. When I turned around, I saw Rafael lying on the ground, knocked out. My other guys had run across to the other side of Lehigh. I was running to them, but when I saw Rafael down and ready to be stabbed by two of the guys, I went back to get him. I got in their way and started hitting them with the cane in my hand. Suddenly, I was being stabbed. I saw the knife hit the side of my chest by my heart. I felt the knives hit my backbone and my neck. As these two guys were stabbing me, I kept swinging from side to side trying to get away from them.

When I finally fell on the ground, I somehow took the cane I had in my hand and swung it so hard that it hit one of the guys in his hand. It looked as if it was broken, and the knife flew out of his hand. Then I was able to get up and hit the other guy with the cane, and he started to run. As they ran, the other five guys who were with me came back and saw that my coat was all cut up. They said I must have been "stabbed all up" because they had seen how the two guys came after me. They kept telling me to leave Rafael because he was dead. But he wasn't; he was just knocked out.

I was so drunk and felt so hot from coming that close to death that I almost fainted. When they picked me up, thinking I had been stabbed, they took off my leather coat. It had three holes over my heart, four in the neck, and ten in the back. After they took off my T-shirt, it was apparent I didn't have one wound in my body. We couldn't believe it. All I remember was Lemon telling me that someone was with me. He said, "To be stabbed so many times and not have a wound in your body, someone big must be with you." I almost thought it was the spirit of the Indian, the one to whom my parents lit candles.

Death faced me so many times that I got to the point where I didn't fear it anymore. I actually was looking for someone to do me the favor of killing me. I hated everyone, including myself. I didn't have peace in my life. People didn't know what I was going through inside at night. Every time I went to sleep, I had terrible nightmares. Each time I was on the corner, fear told me every car that drove by held someone about to shoot me. I feared every time I was at a discotheque that somebody would shoot me or stab me from behind while I was there.

But no one knew this. No one knew that when I went home at night I would have to leave the radio on because I was scared to have too much silence. I came to a point where I really wanted to get out of this kind of life. However, when I thought back on the reputation I had as the leader of the Midtown Zulu gang, all these young guys looking up to me and many others wanting to join the gang, I figured this was the only life I could live.

My brother Philip and his common-law wife, Mae, had broken up. I loved Mae because she was almost like a mother to me. She gave us money and treated Debbie and me as if we were her own children. When Mae and Philip separated, they left us the house. Richie, number two in my gang, moved in with us. At times, Mae would come by and get the bills to pay them; we didn't have to pay anything to

66

stay there, and we were there for almost six months.

One day Richie, Debbie, and I were smoking marijuana and drinking wine. I had a shotgun we had named Sweet Susie on my lap. Debbie was sitting on the stereo speaker when the phone rang. We told Debbie to get up and answer the phone. She didn't want to, but finally she got up and walked to the phone. It was her boyfriend, Chris. As soon as she got up to walk away, Richie and I decided we wanted to stand up too. But we were so drunk that we fell back down. As we fell, the shotgun went off and put a hole in the wall just above the speaker where Debbie had been sitting. If it had been thirty seconds earlier, Debbie would have been dead. The hole was at least eight inches in diameter. We tried to hide it so that Philip and Mae wouldn't see it. Meanwhile, we decided to wait for Chris to go out with us and buy some more wine.

3rd & Diamond and Midtown Zulu Gang 1974

Mikey

Debbie, Chris, Richie, and I went to get the wine after they had hustled for the money. Walking down the street, we arrived at Fifth Street and Allegheny Avenue and found some other guys who were walking south on Fifth. We were going north and began to argue about who was going to go on the sidewalk first. This was something very stupid to be fighting about. A fight broke out with these guys, and we started chasing them down the street.

As I was chasing this guy, he turned back and hit me on the head with a bottle, but I hit him twice with a cane; so he left me alone. I don't even know where the people came from. Several got out of their cars and were fighting us. Someone yelled out to my brother Mikey that I had blood on my face and had been shot. While attempting to save me, Mikey got hit on his chest and fell. When he fell, the guy who had hit him struck him on the head and crushed his skull.

I ran home to get the double-barreled, sawed-off shotgun, Sweet Susie. As I came back with it, somebody yelled out that Mikey was dead. When I heard that, I started crying, but they were not tears of hurt. My brother Mikey was just lying there with no life in his body. He was carried to a clinic on Fifth and Cambria Streets. Suddenly, the cops were all over the place, arresting everyone. They arrested about thirty of our guys, and they also arrested the guys we fought. I wasn't arrested that day, but the police were looking for me. That night my parents and Philip told me to turn myself in. But I didn't.

I couldn't sleep because I was thinking about Mikey. I couldn't believe he was gone. When he died, I died with him. I made a promise to kill people until I got the person who had killed my brother. The cops finally found me, but three days later my father paid a fifteen-thousand-dollar bond to get me out of jail. I was also being charged with two attempted murders for the other two guys who were stabbed that day.

When I got home, I still couldn't believe Mikey was dead. Although I was crying, I was also very angry. I loaded my shotgun with two shells, put it in a briefcase, and walked down the street. I was nicely dressed because I didn't want to look suspicious. I went to a friend's house where Little Hawk and Richie were. They told me, "Joey, don't do anything. Just let it go. Let it rest for a while. Let's bury your brother. We'll take care of business later." But I didn't want to hear that. I started to cry, and I was very angry. I just wanted to kill someone.

The next day we started collecting money on Fifth and Indiana for the funeral expenses. We raised fifteen hundred to two thousand dollars. Many people helped us out, including people who didn't know him. We gave my mother the money because she couldn't afford to bury him. Now she had the money for the burial ground and everything else. I remember when we went to the viewing. I walked in, and as soon as I saw Mikey in the casket, I grabbed him, put my face on his chest, and started to cry so loudly that no one else could come in for a while. My mother and all my brothers and sisters were crying too.

My father just stood there. I remember him saying, "The one who said he was going to kill me when he turned eighteen, look where he is today." Then he sat down. I stared at my father and couldn't believe what I was hearing. There was no pain, no remorse, and no sympathy for my brother Mikey. As I cried on my brother's chest, I said, "Mikey, I'll get revenge on your death."

The next day, we buried my brother. Again, I knelt down by his grave and said, "Mikey, if I have to kill fifty people to get revenge for your death, I will kill them. Someone is going to pay for your death."

A few weeks after my brother died, my mother started to blame me for his death. She started to curse me,

69

telling me that Mikey was dead because of me. She told me I was worse than he was and said, "He was never like you." But she didn't know anything about Mikey. She always knew about me because I was the one who always had to leave home, the one who had to live in the streets, and the one who was always on drugs. She didn't know that by telling me these things she was killing me right along with Mikey. She destroyed me completely. I was already feeling that I wasn't myself anymore. I could talk, and it wasn't me. I could walk and it wasn't me. I felt as if I didn't own myself any more. Whoever did own me was having a party with my life; they were having their way with me all the time.

Thirty days after we buried Mikey, two friends of mine, Lefty and Country, came and told me that they had some problems. They asked me to go with them to help them out, and in return they would help me to obtain revenge for Mikey's death. I got my shotgun. They had another guy with them, Carlos, who was supposed to get his gun too. But I told them that if they were going to bring him, I wasn't going. I had had a confrontation with him in the past about my brother's death. So we left him.

We got into a station wagon, and there was a girl with them. I didn't even know her name. We walked into the neighborhood and stuck the shotgun down the girl's overalls. We walked right to the corner where many people were outside. All I remember was letting both barrels go and several people falling to the ground. When they fell, I turned around and started to run. About nine had fallen.

Earlier, Country told me I wasn't going to shoot any one. I told him, "Once I kill all these people, I'm going to come back and kill you." I reloaded the gun, stuck it in Country's face, and asked him, "Now, what did you say?"

He replied, "Man, you are crazy. Take that thing out of my face!" He pulled the gun away from his face, and then I put it away. Lefty told me to get out of there. As soon as we left, all we saw were cops swarming the corner where I had

70

shot those people. When I got home that night, I realized the shotgun had ripped my hand somewhat. The following day, I learned that nine people had been shot. Later I heard in the news that none of them died.

When they told me I had shot nine people, I fled to an abandoned house. I was trying to stay out of the neighborhood because the cops were looking for everyone. All the guys from our gang were being arrested. I was in this abandoned house with Richie, drinking wine when I started to cry. I told him I was tired of life. "Why do I go around hurting people? Why can't I be like normal people? Why can't I have peace? Why do I have to live such a terrible life?" I was so miserable that I kept on crying.

But my tears weren't tears of remorse. They were tears of anger and hurt. I was angry with myself, and I hated myself. I called my father and told him that I had shot so many people; he told me to be quiet about it and to not say anything. My own father had given me the shotgun that I used to shoot all those people. He had told me that if I didn't use it, he would use it on me. That night, I couldn't sleep. I could only think about those people who were hurt, the cops searching all over the place for me, and everyone being investigated.

Prison

Suddenly, I started hearing voices in my mind telling me, "Joey, you shot and killed people. If there is a God in heaven, Joey, he'll never forgive you. God doesn't forgive people who kill." I had no peace. I went to Phoenixville, Pennsylvania for a couple of days with Philip and my cousin Carmelo, who lived there. We got drunk, and Carmelo told me there was a gun store down the street. He asked me if I wanted to go down there to steal some guns.

I told Carmelo I wasn't going to be satisfied until I

71

killed the guy — or some member of his family — who killed my brother. After playing pool, we went down the street to the Army-Navy store. The owner tried to grab me when he saw me stealing some knives, but I hit him with a pair of boots and threw him through the window, almost killing him. When I finally got outside, it seemed like the entire Phoenixville Police Department was waiting for me. I was ready to start shooting, but I froze because I realized my gun didn't have any bullets. Still I tried to get away from them knowing there was no way out.

When they apprehended me, I fought and cursed them, but they finally subdued me and put me in the car. At the police station, they put the handcuffs on me so tight that I started to curse them again. I started to get very sick from the liquor. Drinking whisky all day without eating anything caused me to throw up. I became very wild. When they finally subdued me and put me in a cell, all I could hear were the voices telling me, "Joey, if there is a God in heaven, He'll never forgive you because God doesn't forgive people who have shot and killed people. Joey, take your life."

This voice repeated itself over and over again. I figured since I was going to be in jail for twenty to thirty years or maybe the rest of my life, why should I live? The voices kept yelling in my mind, telling me to kill myself. I was so fed up and frustrated that I took off my coat and tied it tightly to the cell bars. Then I took the other side and tied it around my neck. The next thing I knew, I was dangling from the cell bars, and everything turned black. Later my brother Philip told me a cop found me hanging from the cell bars and cut the coat down.

The police took me to Emorysville State Hospital, a mental facility, for a week. There I was evaluated by a group of professionals: psychiatrists and social workers. They put me in a room and asked me why I had committed those crimes and why I tried to kill myself. I just kept chewing on a straw, looking to the ceiling. I wasn't crazy, but I felt as if I were becoming crazy, watching all those people. I was losing my mind just by being there.

The psychiatrist told my mother that I had a very violent temper, and under pressure I was liable to kill any one. He also told her I needed psychiatric treatment, saying, "If he ever gets out of here, he needs to see a psychiatrist." My mother told the doctor about my brother's death. She figured it was probably the reason I was going through all of this because he had been killed in front of me.

From that mental hospital I was sent to the Chester County Prison in West Chester, Pennsylvania. I had three open cases there and many cases open back in Philadelphia. I was taken from one place to another. First, I was held in the Philadelphia Detention Center for awhile. Then I was moved back to the Chester County Prison. I expected to be in jail for at least twenty to thirty years of my life.

It Had to Be an Angel

After I was in the Chester County Prison for two months, a guard came to my cell. I had never seen him before. When he came up to me, he looked straight at me and called me by name. The whole time he was talking to me, I kept asking myself why I had never seen him before. I was very puzzled by it. He was dressed just like all the other guards, yet there was something very distinctive about him.

He told me I was going to get out of jail. He also said that many of my charges were being dropped and that I was going to receive time served and walk out. I thought he was crazy and told him he didn't know what he was talking about. After he stopped speaking, he looked at me intensely and then spoke again, "Joey, you're going to get out of this prison, but remember this: Jesus Christ is there with you all the days of your life. He loves you. He loves you, Joey." And he walked away.

When he said that, I cursed and yelled out to him, "I don't believe in God. No one can forgive me! There is no God in heaven who can forgive me." But it seemed that as I was speaking, it wasn't really me. It was as if there was another person inside of me speaking; I was so angry when he said that.

The guard spoke to me on Monday; by Friday I was released from prison. When the guards called me, I was in the cafeteria. They said, "José Perez, F-24 discharged." I thought I was going to be there for a long time. So they asked me again, "Are you José Perez, F-24?" I said yes. They told me there was no mistake. I was being discharged. I almost couldn't believe I was being released as I walked out of prison. Today, I believe that guard was an angel sent by God to speak to my life.

When everyone found out I was coming home, Richie, Little Man, Lemon, and Gun came to my house to see me. They were amazed and shocked to see me out. They told me they never expected me to be released. I told them that someone was with me. I didn't know who it was, but there I was, free again. We got extremely drunk at the welcoming party they held for me.

About two weeks later, my sisters Evelyn, Gigi, and Debbie, and their friend Deedee, a beautiful black woman, invited me to go to a party with them. We went to a discotheque on Tenth Street and Erie Avenue called The Towney. As we arrived, Little Man and Slap came up to me and said, "Joe, some guys here want to talk to you." Upon walking over to them, I found out they were from a rival gang called Fifteenth and Venango. They quickly broke bottles, pulled out knives, grabbed chairs, and pulled out guns. At first, I thought Little Man and Slap had framed me. Later I found out that they had been deceived into believing the gang was friendly.

The guys from the gang asked me if I was the leader of my gang. This thought came to my mind: "If I'm going to die, I'm going to die tough, and someone is going with me!" So I pushed the guy who asked me and said, "Yes, I am the leader of this gang." Then I hit him. When he fell, I started swinging punches everywhere. I became very wild, yelling, "Kill me! Kill me! I'm not scared to die! Kill me!"

Suddenly, they backed off and said, "Man, we've never seen a Puerto Rican as crazy as you!"

I told them, "My brother has just been killed, and I am ready to die too! I hate life! If you have the heart, you can kill me right now!" Turning, I walked out of there. I thought that as soon as I turned my back someone would shoot or stab me, but no one did. I went outside and found Little Man and Slap. They didn't know what had happened to me inside the club. My anger caused me to punch both of them and tell them to stay out of my face. Then I walked away.

How could I have walked away from something so dangerous without being hurt? I started to think again that perhaps someone was with me. Every day I thought about all the times that I had been close to death yet never got shot or stabbed. I tried to figure out who was with me, thinking that perhaps it was the spirit of the Indian whom my mother talked about and to whom she lit candles. But I didn't believe too much in that either.

Chapter 9

A New Business

About two weeks later, Philip got a job at a factory on Second and Lippincott Streets, where my cousin Johnny was working. The same factory hired me also. We would get paid and then spend all our money on drugs. I wanted to stay out of trouble, but I was still hanging out with the guys. Philip was very dominating and controlling. He would smack me around a couple of times, even though I was eighteen-years-old. One day he smacked my friends and me in the face because he didn't want me to hang around them. They were afraid of my brother.

The next time I saw my mother I told her, "Philip thinks I am a little boy. When I was younger, he could smack me in the face, and I would take it. But when I was in jail, I didn't let anyone, big or little, take advantage of me. I don't take anything from anyone in the streets, and I am not scared of Philip anymore. If he hits me again, I am going to hurt him! So you had better tell him to leave me alone."

My mother remembered what the psychiatrist advised her concerning my violent temper; he had told her that under pressure I was liable to kill someone. That night she told my brother Philip to leave me alone, saying, "Joey is not scared of you, and you are just pressuring him to hurt you."

One night after hanging out with the guys on the corner, I went home. After awhile, Philip walked in the house. He came right up to me and punched me in the eye. Before he could swing the second punch, I caught his arm in my hand and hit him ten times. Then I dragged him outside and threw him over a car before he knew what had hit him. When Philip realized what I had done, he was shocked. I told him, "Boy, I am not scared of you, and if you ever try to hit me again, I am going to kill you."

When he looked in my eyes, he knew I meant

business. Philip was three years older than I was. He always went around cutting people, and many people hated him. Philip knew I had committed more violent crimes than he ever had. He also knew that I would fight anybody and that I wasn't a little boy anymore. I was growing up, and I wasn't going to let him take advantage of me. For the most part, Philip left me alone. Sometimes he aggravated me, but I didn't want to hurt him. I stopped working at the factory and began hanging out and getting high with the guys down in the neighborhood.

My sister Evelyn had rented a house on Orianna and Cambria Streets. My mother was moving out and buying a house on American and Westmoreland Streets. I still didn't get along with my mother's husband. I tried to kill him three times; once I stuck a gun in his mouth. Another time, while he was sleeping, I stole a thousand dollars from him. Seeing this, my mother fell on her knees and started to cry, asking me why I didn't let her live in peace. My hand was loaded with a thirteen-inch dagger ready to kill him.

My mother was always putting him first and rejecting me. She begged me to kill her instead. She was tired of the things I was doing to her husband. I even thought about stabbing my mother a couple of times. I had a great deal of anger toward her, but then I was angry with everyone any way. I blamed my parents for the miserable life I lived because they had brought me into this world.

This is why my mother finally decided to buy another house and move out of the neighborhood. I moved in with my sister Evelyn at 2915 N. Orianna Street. After being with her for a while, I found a job. My brother-in-law, Tarzan, my sister Gigi's husband, found a job for me at a dental factory on Twenty-first and Clearfield Streets. However, I was still in trouble. Messing up again, I realized that sooner or later I was going to end up back in prison.

Because it was wintertime, the gang was calmer, even though we were partying quite a bit. The gang wars

77

were starting to die out. I told the guys who came to my house to get high that I wasn't going to be their leader any more. They weren't too thrilled about it, but there wasn't anything they could do. I was crazy anyway, and they didn't want to bother with me.

With less than a month until I was off probation, my probation officer was trying to put me back in jail because I was still getting into trouble. Although I didn't care about my job, I stayed there for about six months.

4th & Huntingdon and Midtown Zulu Gang 1975

Drug Dealing

There was a guy named Mike at the dental factory where I worked. The factory handled mescaline and other chemicals that could be used to make cocaine, and Mike knew about them. We stole some of the materials to make drugs. I started selling marijuana and cocaine. Mike introduced me to several of his gangster friends who hung out at El Dorado's Bar on Broad and Erie Avenues and at the

Fishnet Bar on Broad and Olney Avenues. I then met some black brothers who were into drugs.

Many of these guys were cold-blooded gangsters. They were mean looking and tried to put fear into my heart, but it didn't work. Because they knew Mike, we started to become friends. They bought from me, and I bought from them. I was making quite a bit of money, and at the same time, my sister Evelyn started selling amphetamines called Monster as well. She too made a great deal of money. From the money she got for drugs, she bought all kinds of things for her house. Sometimes I would even go to pick up drugs for her from a lady we called Mom. I would bring it to Evelyn, and she would bag it up and sell it.

After doing this for some time, Evelyn was held up by some guys who had supposedly been friends. They came to her house when she wasn't at home, tied up Cuchi and another guy who was there, took her children, and stuck guns in their faces. My little niece Millie was about five-years old. These guys told Cuchi that if she didn't tell them where the drugs were, they were going to kill the children.

But they only found a few drugs and left. After this incident, Evelyn became nervous about her drug business. Her big mistake was calling the cops, who immediately began watching her. They knew something was wrong and wondered why someone would want to hold her up unless she was doing something illegal.

When we found out about this, Blueberry, Philip, the guys from the gang, and I went on a rampage looking for these three guys. One of them was so scared that he got himself arrested because he knew we were going to kill him. I found out later that another one had been found burned to death and shot in the chest with a shotgun. How that happened I don't know. I caught the last one on Fourth and Indiana Streets. I beat him so badly that even the guys who were on the corner with him would not jump in to help him.

They knew that if they tried to help him there would be a major war in that neighborhood.

Big Money

From that day on, I took over Evelyn's business. I sold amphetamines, marijuana, and cocaine. I was also racketeering with Mike and his friends on Broad Street and doing gun and rifle transactions. I was able to make enough money to buy my own drugs to sell. After awhile, I bought nice clothes and a new car. When teenagers saw me with new cars, nice clothes, and plenty of money, they wanted to sell drugs for me. So I gave them drugs to sell.

I also got my sister Debbie and her husband Chris to sell drugs for me on Twentieth Street. A bunch of the old heads in the neighborhood sold for me as well. I provided everybody with drugs. Izzy, Shake & Bake, Judge, Georgie, his wife, and Tati were also helping me sell drugs. I was making big money in the drug business. I had teenagers selling marijuana and opium around Indiana Street and adults selling cocaine and amphetamines.

As fast as I made the money, I spent it. I was always giving people money and helping people in need. If any wife of a friend needed something for the children, I would give her money. I bought clothes and new shoes for many of my friends, especially for those who hung around me. I dressed them up, and every time we went to a discotheque I bought them a new outfit so that they could go looking clean. I didn't care how expensive the clothes were. I started getting all my own clothes tailor-made. I had a guy who made all my suits and pants, and I bought my shirts through catalogues.

Even with all of this, I still had no peace and no joy. I was miserable, and I was still having terrible nightmares. When you are a drug dealer, you always have problems. Sometimes you want to kill some of your drug dealers

80

because they short you on your money. You have to hurt them so that other dealers won't even think about doing the same thing. Sometimes you even have to kill them to teach the rest a lesson and to keep your reputation intact.

Even though I was making lots of money from selling drugs, I was very unhappy. The cops kept watching me, and sometimes they would take me to the police station and beat me up. They hated me. They knew that I was a big troublemaker in the community and that I had a lot of drug activity going on, but they couldn't find anything.

One day after being locked up overnight, I came out of the police station all beaten up. My lip and nose were broken. The cops had a party with me the night before! They were trying to find out where I was getting my money and all my new possessions. They knew I did not have a job but was still buying plenty of new things. The cops released me early that morning, and I found Rick on the corner.

I told him what had happened to me, and he told me to get a job where he worked. He said, "Look, Joe, why don't you go there to see if you can get hired? Use this job as an escape! Having a job before helped you to keep the cops off your back. Maybe it will still work for you." I thought it was a good idea.

That same night we all got high. I really wanted to open up to Rick and share with him what was in my heart. But it was so hard for me to do that because I never told anyone what was inside me. As we were getting high, I said to him, "Rick, I am tired of life. I am tired of everything. Every night I think of killing myself. I am scared to go to sleep, and sometimes I am even scared to wake up because this life has become a living hell to me. I never have peace when I walk down the streets or when I go to sleep. You know, Rick, if I didn't have anything but peace, that's all I would want in life."

Rick replied, "I don't understand you, Joey. Everyone respects you! You have nice things — a nice car and plenty of money. You can go anywhere, and people respect you. Now you're telling me that you are miserable?" I told Rick that I'd rather have nothing — no money, no material things — I just wanted to have peace because I hated the life I lived. I wanted to break down and cry, but I couldn't do it because of my reputation. I got up and told him I would see him in the morning. I wanted to go to this job he was talking about. Maybe something good would come out of it.

Chapter 10

Divine Destination

I didn't know God was already in the middle of all this. The God of the heavens and the earth had a plan for me at this company, and I was totally unaware of it.

After I got home that night, I lay in bed thinking about my life and about how miserable I was. My thoughts focused on killing my mother and my little sister so that they wouldn't have to suffer anymore; then I would kill myself. I was also thinking about killing four of my drug dealers who were already behind in bringing my money! Two joints of marijuana gave me a high that enabled me to get a superficial peace and go to sleep.

I woke up at five in the morning because I had to meet Rick at six on Second Street and Allegheny Avenue. My mother asked me where I was going. I told her I was going to see about a job with Rick. She replied that she hoped I would find a job because at least that would keep me out of trouble. I left the house and stood on the corner waiting for Rick. When he pulled up, I noticed he had three other guys in the car with him. Looking closer, I realized one of them was a guy who didn't like me, but I didn't have a grudge against him. They probably didn't like me because of my bad reputation.

One of them, named Victor, lived on Fourth and Indiana and was a very jealous man. He thought everyone on the corner was trying to steal his wife. Many times he upset me with his jealousy; I wasn't interested in his wife, although I thought about doing something with her just to give him a reason to be jealous! But later we became good friends. He realized his insecurity made him think everyone was trying to hit on his wife.

I didn't know the other two guys in the car. They were very husky and looked like body builders. They never got high at all. But Victor, Rick, and I started to smoke marijuana all the way to the job site on Norcom Road by Roosevelt Boulevard. The company's name was Cardo's Automobile Productions.

Rick started working at 7:00 a.m., but my interview wasn't until 8:00 a.m. As I walked through the doors, I already felt that I wasn't going to like the place. I kept getting thoughts in my mind about leaving. The guards by the doors asked me to show them some identification and then told me to go into a particular room. Going in, I realized that there were three other guys already waiting: an Irish guy named Johnny, a black guy, and another Hispanic guy.

I started to talk with the Hispanic guy, but he didn't know much English; I certainly didn't know much Spanish! I tried to talk to him the best I could. Even though I am Puerto Rican, born and raised in Philadelphia, my Spanish at that time wasn't the greatest. As we were talking, a man walked in. He looked at me and kept staring at me. I started to feel very uneasy with this guy. I had a big Afro, and I had stuck some marijuana in my hair. I figured he could probably see it, so as he continued to stare at me, I stared back at him. Then he asked me, "What did you come here for?"

Revealing my bad attitude, I responded, "What do people come to a factory for when they don't have a job?"

And he said, "I don't know." I couldn't tell if he was being smart or sarcastic. In a nasty tone of voice I told him I was there because I was looking for a job. At this point, I didn't care if I was hired or not. All of a sudden, this guy started to smile, and this upset me even more. I thought he was trying to make me look like a fool. He just kept on smiling and took the applications that had been given to us when we went into the room.

He was the personnel manager at Cardo's, and his name was Carl Moline. He began calling us one by one. I was the last one to be called. Bringing me into his office, he started to ask me a number of questions. When I had filled out the application, there had been a part on it that asked if I had ever committed a felony. I put down everything for which I had ever been convicted. I even turned the application around and filled out the other side too. I figured by doing that I wouldn't get hired.

Carl Moline hummed as he reviewed my application. When he got to the last part, he kept saying, "Uh, huh, this is very interesting." Then he looked at me and asked if I had ever been arrested.

I answered, "Well, what does my application say?" He told me then that I had a very interesting story. He realized that when I was in the government program, I had graduated from a body and fender course. He also saw that I had a cooking and restaurant certificate. Then he asked me if I knew how to paint, and I told him yes.

He said, "Good, because we need a painter. Right now, however, we have an opening in the dismantling department." He told me to come back the next day before 7:00 a.m. to start working; my shift would start at 7:30 in the morning. I felt somewhat strange when he said that. It seemed as if the superficial peace I had left me.

I began feeling really uneasy inside; my body started to tremble. I didn't want to be there. Something wasn't right. So I said to myself, "Maybe this guy is an FBI agent, and maybe Rick is the informant who has been telling the cops that I am the one selling all the drugs. He probably brought me here so that they can trap me!" This guy was smiling too much; he looked like a cop. I didn't know that Carl Moline was a Christian or that what I was thinking about him and about Rick was not true. But my sin haunted me day and night. I always thought someone was trying to "get over" on me or trying to trap me.

I remember the occasion in my past when two women tried to set me up. They lured me into a house, and once I was there, they tried to arrange for me to be killed by some people who wanted me dead. I didn't trust anyone.

People Like You . . .

When I got the job, I told Mr. Moline, "Look, I don't understand. I am a gang leader and a drug dealer. Why is it that you are hiring me when people like you don't hire people like me?" Carl Moline looked at me and smiled again; that smile agitated me.

He said, "Did I ask you what you were or what you have done in the past?" I said no with a nasty attitude. Then he asked, "Why are you asking me these questions? You want a job? Come tomorrow, and you'll start then."

I said to myself, "Something isn't right." But I decided I was going to go back to see what this was all about. I would just have to be very careful of the things I did or said just in case Mr. Moline was an FBI agent and Rick an informant! After the interview, I went home. That evening Rick came to see me, and I told him what had happened. I looked at Rick strangely, thinking something wasn't right with him. I didn't understand back then what was going on. Today, however, I realize that Satan didn't want me in that company, and God was bringing me there because He had a divine purpose in my life to save me.

That night Rick and I got high again. I asked him if he could pick me up in the morning because I was having car problems. He agreed. He came by for me at 6:00 a.m. Even though I didn't start until 7:30 a.m., I went with him anyway. I walked in and was given my ID. I was shown around and assigned to work under a man named Ed Phillips. We called him Big Ed. He was an Irish guy who was so big that he looked as if he could be a Sumo wrestler. He had white hair and looked like a very nice guy.

Ed took me to the water pump department and told me I was going to work there. He showed me what I was going to do and put me at this little machine where I would be until I worked my way up to painting water pumps. The area contained water pumps to be dismantled and sent through machines that cleaned them. My job was to take the pellets and bearings that came out of the water pumps and punch the bearings out of the pellets. He showed me what to do – how to stick the bearings in the pellets on these plates and then step on a little pedal so that a long nail came down and knocked the bearings out.

I had to take the pellets and throw them in a bucket; the bearings would automatically fall in another bucket. The first day I did this job I hated it. It was dirty, greasy work. I wasn't too thrilled with my job and couldn't wait to go to lunch at noon. I wanted to go outside to smoke a joint of marijuana or snort some cocaine. I just wanted to get high.

On my way outside I met a few guys who worked there: Bernard, Peanut, and James. They asked me if I wanted to go with them to smoke some marijuana. Walking out to the parking lot, I realized we weren't the only ones out there. It seemed as if a third of our department was getting high. One guy was shooting up heroin right in the parking lot. Even women were smoking marijuana. When I saw this, I recognized it as a good opportunity for me to sell drugs. I wanted to find out if anyone was already selling drugs in the company because I wanted to take over.

As I talked to Bernard, I told him I was a drug dealer and said, "I don't know who's selling drugs around here, but I have everything you want. I have people on the street selling drugs for me. I can hook up anyone in here who wants to sell some drugs for me. If you want, I can help you make some money on the side." Bernard told me no one was selling drugs there. They were getting drugs from white guys who worked on the other side of the company. They really didn't want to do business with them because the Irish and the Italians working there were selling a bunch of junk.

I gave them a taste of what I had, and they liked it. The next day when I came to work, they ordered some drugs from me, and I told them to pay me on Friday. I told Bernard, Peanut, and James that maybe they could sell drugs for me too. They told me they wouldn't mind. I told them I had opium, hash, marijuana, cocaine, heroin, amphetamines, rifles, and guns. Anything they wanted, I could get for them to sell.

I found a couple of guys in the water pump and brake department to sell drugs for me. I had Rick in the carburetor department. From then on, I started to like the job. I found I could make more money there than I did on the streets. Even though the job was a dirty one, the money was rolling in pretty well.

After being there for thirty days, I noticed these two short Italian guys standing behind me, watching me. Every day from Monday through Friday, they would stand behind me for a few hours. They kept watching me work.

On the other side of the company was the caliper department. A husky Italian man who looked like the Hulk was that department's manager. He looked tough like a slave driver. One day he walked over to me and told me he needed a couple of guys to work in his department. His name was Cozzy, and he asked me if I would like to put in some overtime. I figured I could give them a couple of days, but once I got in the union I wouldn't work overtime any more. I wanted to get in the union because I started liking the job due to all the money I was making selling drugs.

I told Cozzy I would put in the overtime he needed. I worked in the caliper department for about four days straight. I noticed that even though Cozzy looked tough, he always had a big smile on his face. He was a nice guy. He would talk to me kindly in a deep, strong voice. Somehow he reminded me a lot of myself.

New Assignment

Every morning, however, for two weeks those short Italian men kept watching me. I worked there for only six weeks and was already in the union. I knew I had a secure job, and they couldn't put me out now; I stopped working the overtime.

But those men continued to stand behind me. I didn't realize these two Italian men were the owners of the company. They and another man, Charlie Hamilton, would stand behind me to watch me work. Charlie was Irish, an older man in his sixties with red hair and freckles. I thought the two Italians were cops; maybe they were watching me because someone had snitched on me. Just their presence tormented me.

One day I became so uncomfortable as they watched me that I grabbed a pipe to hit them. However, all they wanted was to talk to me. They had me turn off my machine so that I could listen to them. One of them said, "I understand you were a foreman at another company before you came here."

"Yeah, so what?" I replied.

"I see you have a lot of ability. You're fast, and you have potential. We think you have a pretty good future here in this company."

When he said that, I told him I wasn't interested in anything but just trying to make an honest living. Of course, I wasn't there to make an *honest living*! I liked the job because I was making good money selling drugs.

One of the owners persisted, "We've read your application, and it states that you have a diploma in body and fender. And you're also a cook! We don't need a cook, but we could use a good painter. I just wanted to tell you that you're doing a good job. As a matter of fact, we've been thinking about moving you to another area in our company."

When he told me that, I became angry; I didn't say anything, but how I felt was reflected on my face. I asked him what he meant, and he told me he would like to send me to Cardo's warehouse to teach me to classify all kinds of motor parts. This would give me a very good salary.

But I told them I wasn't interested in another position. I liked where I was now. The owner asked me, "Why don't you want to go? You could make more money!"

The reason I didn't want to go — which I couldn't tell him — was that I couldn't keep an eye on the drug transactions I had going on at the company. My drug business would go straight down the drain.

He told me he was going to send me anyway. I argued that I didn't have a high school diploma. I didn't know how to read well; my schooling had been juvenile homes, prisons, mental hospitals, and government programs. I told him he really didn't want to send me. "Send somebody with a college degree!" I said.

Despite my excuses, the owner just looked me in the eyes, grabbed my hand and with a big smile on his face, said, "You know, we're going to send you! We believe that you can learn the job and that you have the potential to do it well." They kept smiling; I was upset. The company's owners told me that the next morning I was to go to Byberry Road and Roosevelt Boulevard.

The next morning I was not at all happy. In fact, I was upset and frustrated. Before I went to my new job site, I stopped at the main building and told a couple of the guys who sold drugs for me that I wasn't going to be working in that department anymore. I had been transferred to another area. If they needed drugs, all they had to do was call me, and I would bring what they wanted to them. I thought this would work.

When I reported to the building on Byberry Road, there were already twenty-four other guys working there. This was a big warehouse. I had some paperwork from the main building to give to the foreman. As I walked in, I yelled loudly, "Who's the boss here?"

It was still early; people were sitting around because it wasn't time to start work yet. As I spoke, all eyes turned to me.

"What are you looking at? Where's the boss in this place?"

An employee named Benny heard me and commented, "Oh boy, what did they send us here? Cozzy is in for a big surprise!"

He went to the intercom to page the foreman; when the foreman arrived, I recognized him as the same husky man I had met a few weeks earlier. This was Cozzy. He had a big smile on his face, remembering me from the main building due to all the overtime I had put in for him.

"Hey, how are you doing, Joe?" But then he realized I was angry. I took my papers and threw them at him; he caught them on his chest with both hands. "What in the world is wrong with you?" he asked in surprise. My answer was to tell him to just hurry up and show me what to do.

I told him, "I didn't want to come here, but they sent me anyway. Now, what do you want me to do? I don't want to be here; I want to go back to the main building. So try to find a way to get me back there." I wasn't upset about the change of location. I was upset because of my drug business in the other building; I knew if I didn't keep an eye on it, I would eventually lose it.

Cozzy looked at me and told me we weren't going to start work for another fifteen minutes. I could go ahead and have a cup of coffee if I wanted. But I just sat there next to an older guy named Julio, who lived near my neighborhood on Fairhill and Cambria. For lack of anything better to do, I began to talk to him. He started to tell me that it wasn't that bad to work there and that I shouldn't worry about it. I told him to shut up. I didn't want to hear anything about the job.

Later, I found out that Julio was a Christian. He used phrases such as, "to God be the glory." It seemed as if every other thing he said was "glory to God!" Julio made me very uncomfortable, and I already knew I wasn't going to like him or anything else about working in the warehouse.

Chapter 11

Increasingly Miserable

When the bell to start work finally rang, Cozzy took me to where I would be working. My job was to take an aluminum water pump and put some type of paste on it that would make a cast around the pump. If the water pump were badly damaged, this cast would make it like new. I didn't like this job at all, although the smell of the liquid paste was so strong that I was already getting high from it.

Frustrated, I worked with absolutely no interest or desire. During our break, I received a phone call from Bernard, telling me that his friends needed some drugs. I told them I would come by at lunch to bring them.

During our lunch break, I went to the other building; because I still had my ID, the guard let me in. Pretending I was going there to get my lunch, I dropped off the drugs and went back to Byberry. I continued to do this for two or three months.

Our afternoon break came at two; Cozzy approached me from behind. He called me by name, but because I didn't hear him coming, I jumped nervously. "Man, what do you want? Don't come up behind me like that!" Cozzy looked at me, smiling, and said he wanted to ask me a question.

He began by commenting, "You look like you're mad at the whole world."

Angrily, I responded, "Look! If I *am* mad at the whole world, what difference does it make to you! As a matter of fact, I don't like you. I don't like any of the guys in this warehouse. If you send me back to the main building, it will make this a better place to work for all of you. But if you keep me here, you'll have problems with me because I don't take anything from anyone!"

Cozzy was patient. He continued to look at me and then said, "Joe, I would like to ask you another question." I told him to hurry up with the questions and get out of my face because I had work to do. So he asked his question. "Joe, do you know that Jesus Christ died on the cross for your sins?"

I just looked at him and thought to myself, "Oh man, what is *wrong* with this guy? Is he crazy? He can't be a religious guy! He looks too mean, too rough looking."

So I asked him, "What are you, one of those religious guys who talk about God?"

"No, I am a Christian," he told me.

I warned him, "Whatever you do, don't talk to me about God! I don't believe in God, and I don't believe in the devil! I don't even want to *hear* what you have to say."

But he kept talking. "Joe, let me ask you one more question. Do you believe Jesus Christ died on the cross to save you from your sins and shed his blood to clean you of your sins?"

"Hey, look!" I told him. "I don't want to hear what you have to say; so shut up and leave me alone! If you don't shut up, I am going to hang *you* on the cross, and *you'll* be the one shedding blood!" Even though I had mocked his God in such a diabolical way, Cozzy just smiled at me.

"Joe, I am going to leave you alone, but before I leave, I want to say something else to you. Did you know the four owners of this company are four Italian brothers who are Christians?" I told him I didn't know that. He continued, "The main building has about eight hundred to a thousand employees, and at least 350 people are born-again Christians."

I interrupted him, "Why are you telling me all this? I don't care who's a Christian and who's not!"

He acted as if I hadn't said a word. "There's one more thing I want to tell you. There are twenty-five people who work in this warehouse with you, and twelve of us are Christians." I told him they had better leave me alone and not try to preach this Jesus stuff to me. "Joe, do you see that little room there? Well, every morning we go to that room to pray. And as of today, we're going to pray for you, Joe. We're going to pray that God saves you."

I threatened Cozzy, "You had better start praying that God saves *you* from me. I am going to kill the first one who tries to preach this Jesus stuff to me! I don't want to hear anything about God."

Cozzy began to walk away from me, but when he was about twenty-five feet away, he turned around, looked me straight in the eye, and said with a big smile on his face, "Joe, Jesus loves you." Then he walked away.

Oh, he aggravated me with that! That day when I got home, I told Rick what had happened.

Fast Money

Every day after work I went to the bar on Fourth and Indiana Streets, where I sold drugs and met a number of people in the community selling for me. I told Rick that the owners at Cardo's had sent me to work in the warehouse. Because of that, I couldn't keep an eye on my drug business anymore. I wanted him to watch my dealers for me. Rick said he would do the best he could to help me but couldn't guarantee anything. Even though I had a decent job, I continued to live the same old way, selling drugs and racketeering. I was just using my job as a cover up. What I didn't know, however, was that God had placed me at Cardo's for a divine purpose. He had a plan for my life, and I wasn't even aware of it.

One day a friend of mine named Louie came to see me. He was one of the old heads from my gang. I liked Louie as much as if he were one of my brothers. He was a tough man and a good fighter. He always looked out for us when my brother Philip was in jail. This particular day Louie told me about some Italian guys in South Philadelphia who were going to commit insurance fraud. He knew a black guy who could help me make some fast money from their scam. I was for anything that made big money! Louie asked me if I wanted to meet him, and I said, "Let's go."

The guys who were committing this fraud wanted us to say we had been in an accident. All I had to do was sign some papers, and they would give me a thousand dollars for one lie. They knew they were going to get a lot more money for my lie because they also had a few others saying the same thing. Once everything was over, they would make about $250,000. They told us that later they'd give us some more money. Even though this sounded like a good deal, I told Louie, "Let's go outside for a second. I need to talk to you."

He asked me what was wrong, and I told him, "You see these guys? They're probably from the mob."

Louie replied, "I don't think so. Just because they're Italian doesn't mean they're with the mob. The mob doesn't racketeer with this stuff; it's too small for them."

I thought about sticking them up for the money, but Louie said not to do it because the black guy knew him *and* where he lived. I told Louie that I didn't care; he didn't know me or where I lived. What difference did it make? I told Louie I was going to take the money, but I wasn't going to do any business with them. I was going to burn these guys for the money they had given me. Louie told me if that was the case, I was on my own. He didn't want any part of it.

These guys from South Philly filled out all the necessary papers and gave me some money. I was supposed to come back another day to sign the rest of the papers. After I received the money, Louie and I went back to the bar at Fourth and Indiana. Even though I was only nineteen, the owner didn't say anything about my being there. He was scared of me, and besides, I brought him business. All the guys from the gang, all my drug dealers, and many people who knew me hung out in his bar. When I walked into the bar, no one said anything to me. I wasn't a bully, but every one respected me for what I was — crazy.

I spent a great deal of money in the bar that day. I succeeded in convincing the owner to set up a discotheque on the second floor of his bar. We would run it and bring a lot of money to his business. He thought it was a good idea, especially after we guaranteed it would fill the entire place. We planned to charge a dollar for admission; they would have to pay double for the liquor. The discotheque began to attract guys and girls from the neighborhood. Windy, Shake & Bake, Big Bird, Georgie, and his wife Carmen, showed up and brought other people with them. We packed the second floor every night from Monday through Sunday. I didn't have to ask any girl to dance with me; all I had to do was show up. The girls flocked around me, asking me to dance.

I danced to every kind of music. In fact, I was pretty good on the dance floor! I always dressed nice with tailor-made clothes, and I even designed some of my own clothes. I always had money in my pocket, although the more money I made, the more I gave away.

Life in the Neighborhood

Every time I got paid, I would sign the check over to my mother. In addition to that, I bought her things for the house, such as furniture and stereos. She didn't ask me where I got the money. My mother didn't even know some of the crimes I had committed. She had some idea of what I was doing, but she wasn't completely sure. As long as I came home at night, that's all that concerned her. Every night I got home at two or three in the morning, only to get up at five for work. My mother always walked into my room to make sure I was there.

I think that after Mikey's death she was constantly worried about whether or not I was all right. She told me she

96

felt I was going to be the next one to die, and she would rather see me dead than alive because I had made her suffer so much.

At the bar, all different kinds of people came to buy drugs from me. I sold to both black Muslims and white guys from the northeast side of town. They came from everywhere. But I didn't always make money. Sometimes when my sister Debbie sold drugs for me, she kept my money; I lost more money with her than with anyone else.

I gave all my brothers and sisters money. I looked out for them, helping them out with whatever they needed. Sometimes, if there wasn't a party on the weekend, I would make the party. We would find one of the old heads, such as Johnny, Mike, or Georgie, at the bar and have the party at one of their houses. I would buy a couple cases of beer, bring the drugs, and put it all on the table. Perhaps that's why so many people liked me.

The wives of several of my friends came to me crying the blues about their husbands not giving them any money. I would help them out, but I didn't realize that by giving them money, I had caused them to like me because I was providing for them what their husbands were not. They threw passes at me, but because I respected my friends, I acted as if I didn't know what was going on. Sometimes I had to tell them off and put them in their place. One thing I can say about the gangs is that we were loyal to one another, even if it caused someone's death. Even with all these women around, I still didn't have any peace. Every time I went into the bar, I sat with my back against the wall so that I could watch everyone going in and out.

Sometimes I acted as bartender for the owner; at the same time I'd sell drugs. The owners of the bar — Lupe and his big brother Gabriel — never said anything to us because they knew we were bringing money to their business. Other times a big dance would take place at one of the dance halls, and we would all get together to go. We stuck together, the

97

guys from the gangs and the guys who sold drugs for me. But everywhere we went there was a fight. There was always something exciting going on, and if we weren't fighting we were shooting at someone. We *thought* it was exciting, not realizing it could have meant our deaths.

If someone from our neighborhood got beaten up, everyone joined in to take care of it. We would shoot at people's houses, do drive-by shootings, and move a whole family out of their house or even out of the neighborhood. Our gang had a reputation for violence. With all of my money and possessions, the loyalty of my gang, and the excitement of my life, I was still miserable. Every day I was concerned about being shot or stabbed or killed. My conscience and my sins haunted me day and night. "How will I die?" I wondered. There had been so many attempted murders, so many shootings, and so many crimes.

Every day I thought about all those people I had shot or stabbed, knowing that one day they might turn around and get their revenge by killing me. This thought filled my mind continually. I believed my death would be a horrible one, and I feared it. I could see myself being shot with a shotgun or a machine gun, being stabbed, or being burned to death.

Ever since Mikey had died, the fear of death gripped my life. I wondered where Mikey had gone and what had happened to him. When I saw my brother in his casket, he was so cold, and there was no life left in him. Was he finally at peace? Was there something better than this life I knew? I thought there had to be. Even though I made very good money selling drugs and working at Cardo's, and even though it seemed as if I were living big, all of it was a masquerade.

My life held no peace or joy. There were times I would lie in my bed at home as drunk as I could be and high as a kite. Often I had to take downers or smoke a few sticks of marijuana to go to sleep, and the next morning, I'd have to take amphetamines to wake up. Many nights I would lie there, and all I wanted to do was cry. I wanted to find a friend, someone to whom I could talk, but there was no one. It seemed everyone I knew was living the same kind of life I was.

Richie and I were always together because he was the only one with whom I could share even the smallest part of my heart. I would tell him some of the things I was going through, and I often wanted to cry in front of him. Even though it seemed as if I didn't trust anyone, I trusted Richie more than I did the other guys. I dreamed so many times of changing my life, and I imagined how I would live that new life.

The Rest of the Story

A few weeks went by, and the Italian guys from South Philadelphia started looking for me. They wanted me to sign their papers so that they could complete the insurance fraud; I had no intentions of signing. As a result, they sent some guys dressed in suits to my mother's house and told her they were from an insurance company and needed to talk to me.

They didn't want to talk to me; they wanted to kill me. But I wasn't afraid of them because I wanted to die any way. I wanted someone to kill me, and I figured I'd take a few of them with me when they finally caught up with me. That was my mentality at the time.

For an entire month, the guys from South Philadelphia called my mother's house two or three times a week looking for me. I wouldn't return their calls. My mother became terribly frustrated with their calling our house.

Coming home from work one day, I saw them standing on the porch talking to Philip. He didn't know what was going on because no one knew my business. As he saw me, I waved back at him quickly, trying to alert him not to say anything to them. I drove away. Later that night, I was in Lupe's bar when Philip came in. He asked me what was wrong and who these guys were who had come to the house looking for me. I explained part of what was happening and told him not to worry about them.

I considered killing them the next time they showed up at our house. For some reason, however, they stopped bothering me. Perhaps they had bigger problems to take care of; they just didn't come around any more. Then I heard that Louie had been shot and was in the hospital. I didn't know who had done it — the guys from South Philly or someone else.

Chapter 12

No Peace at All

Even though Philip was my oldest brother, I always sensed that he didn't like me. When we were younger, we got along well, and he always wanted me around him. However, as we got older, that changed. When Philip saw that everyone respected his younger brother, he became very jealous of me, so much so that he would do anything to aggravate me. He even paid his friends to start fights with me. Philip's little group of guys included a bunch of alcoholics who were always drunk on Bacardi. If he sent one of them, the guy received such a whipping that he never considered doing it a second time.

It seemed that whenever I heard about my brother it was because he had cut someone. He scarred so many people's faces with knives that I used to tell him, "You know, one of these days, someone is going to get tired of what you're doing, and they're going to kill you!"

He replied, "Well, I was born to die anyway. Everybody's got to go sometime!"

Philip was always angry. Many times I felt sorry for his wife, Gladys. Before Gladys started dating my brother, I told her, "Listen, I don't think you want to live with my brother. He's crazy."

I remember her reply. "Oh, I'll change him." However, their living together caused her to realize that she was in hell with him. Once he chased her down the street with a 30.30 Winchester, trying to blow her away in front of her children. He practically tortured those children, holding guns to their mother's head and playing Russian roulette with her in front of them. On another occasion, he tried to nail her to the floor. I never saw a man treat any woman so badly.

Brother Against Brother

Philip was so envious that he had a vendetta against me. He wanted to bring me down and didn't care how he did it. There were four guys who always hung out with my brother: Indio, Travis, Johnny, and Luther. One day there was a party at Indio's house, and Philip invited me to come. Because I was a good dancer, they wanted me to dance with some of their girls because the guys didn't know how to dance themselves.

As I was leaving the bar, Indio was walking in. Suddenly, he grabbed me by the throat. Indio was over six feet tall and weighed 280 pounds; he was also a big bully. He pretended he was just roughhousing with me, kicking me in the stomach and dragging me all the way back into the bar. When he kneed me in the stomach, he took all the air out of me, and I was turning blue as he threw me onto a pool table. My nose and mouth were bleeding, but I was able to catch my breath. Then my brother Philip asked him, laughing, "Man, what did you do to my brother?" I remained quiet and went to clean myself up.

Philip went with Indio and the rest of the guys to his house; I got my .25 automatic before going there. When I arrived, Indio was sitting there joking and laughing at me. He stood up to grab me again, but I pulled back. I told him that I would kill him if he ever grabbed me like that again. Then I hit him right in front of his wife and all his friends.

Indio got an ax, but he saw that I wasn't running away. I held my gun to his forehead and told him, "You might be big, but I'll kill you right now in front of everybody here." His wife and the rest pleaded with me not to kill him. Indio froze; he was scared to death.

He fell on his knees before me and begged, "Joey, please don't kill me." I was so angry that I wanted to blow him away. I'm not sure what held me back; perhaps it was the sight of his two little children watching me.

After that, Philip and Indio held up my drug dealers and took all of the money, completely messing up my business. I contemplated sending a couple of guys to kill them; I considered doing this to my own brother. Before I did any thing, however, I decided I would go to my father about Philip. Finding my father at the bar, I told him that I needed to talk to him. When his friends saw me there, they started to buy me whisky. They knew my reputation and figured that if they bought me a drink, I might get them out of trouble sometime.

I didn't want those kinds of friends. I wanted to get out of trouble and get out of this fast life I was living. I used to say, "A new friend today is a new enemy tomorrow." I said to my father, "Look, I am going to tell you right now you had better talk to Philip; because if you don't get his attention, I'm going to kill him. I'll bring him dead to your lap." My father knew how angry I was. I continued, "I don't like what he's doing to me. He's sticking up all of my drug dealers. He's got his friends starting trouble with me. I even feel like killing a couple of them. So you talk to him before I kill him."

My father told me not to be concerned about it; he was going to take care of things. The next time Philip went to my father's bar, my father smacked him around and told him to leave me alone. My father said, "You know, Joey will kill you." He smacked Philip a few more times, and Philip pulled a gun on him. Enraged, my father looked at him and said, "You'll never kill anybody! You're nothing!" Then my father threw him out of the bar.

I was at a point in my life where I was either going to kill a number of people or myself. I made a list of people to kill. Women asked me to kill their husbands. People wanted to pay me five to ten thousand dollars just to kill one of their family members. I seriously thought about doing it, but I couldn't. I wasn't a contract killer.

I met another group of Italian guys from South

Philadelphia. They approached me and said, "Listen, we've heard about you from a friend who used to work with you, a Polish guy named Bob. We'll give you ten thousand for each person you kill. If there's anyone you want to have killed, just let us know, and we'll do it for you. We want these killings to look like a racial thing; we don't want it to look like we did it."

Waiting for Friday

Working at Cardo's, I kept thinking about the other guys — the ones who had gone to my house. They finally got in contact with me; my mother had mistakenly given them my work number. They called, and Cozzy passed the phone to me. They threatened me, saying, "Look, if you don't sign the papers, we're going to kill you. If we can't kill you, we'll kill your mother and your little sister along with anyone else who lives in the house. So you had better sign them. If we don't hear from you by Friday, your family will die!"

This took away the little peace I had. I was terribly worried, especially for my sister Wandy, my brother Willie, and my mother. I got a shotgun to keep at the house and a pistol to carry with me. Every day I thought about the papers, but if I signed them, those guys might kill me anyway. I didn't trust them at all. I decided that if they tried to come to our house early when my brother and sister were there, I would be waiting for them.

During that week, I didn't hang around with my friends after work. Instead, I stayed home with the shotgun under the sofa and the pistol on me. My mother had no idea what was going on or why I wasn't going anywhere. I plotted how to shoot those guys as they walked up on the porch.

Cozzy looked at me on Wednesday as I came in to work and asked, "Joe, can I talk to you?"

I replied, "You know I don't like you. I don't have anything to say to you."

"Joe," he said, "you don't have any peace."

Frequently, Cozzy would say that to me and then tell me that Jesus was the solution to my problems. Each time I heard that, it aggravated me. In the warehouse, all the Christians tried to find a way to talk to me about Jesus. They were working next to me, or I had to work with them. I don't know if Cozzy planned it that way or not, but it certainly looked like it.

Another Christian worked on the job; his name was John Gallashore. He was an ex-drug dealer and ex-gang member from a gang on Twelfth and Poplar Streets. John related to me all the things he had done. As soon as he mentioned the name of his gang, I said, "Yeah, I used to be from Downtown Zulu. We used to gang war with you. Do you want to fight now?"

He looked at me, laughed, and said, "I'm just sharing with you what God has done for me."

I told him I didn't want to know what God had done for him. "God can't change me because there is no God. All that stuff you're talking about is something you did yourself. Stop thinking God did it. God didn't do it."

"No, Joe, Jesus *did* change me. He cleansed me with His blood, and He transformed my life." Suddenly, I became furious and started to curse him. I told him to get away from me because he was getting on my nerves. Then I walked away.

The closer it was to Friday, the less peace I had. I stayed at home. I left for a little while to collect some drug money, but then I'd come right back home.

On Thursday, I got home and sat down to watch the news. The shotgun still rested under the sofa by the front door, and the pistol was on me. The news carried a story about four Italian guys and a black guy who had just been arrested for insurance fraud. As I watched, I thought, "Hold up! These are the guys who were looking for me."

The cops had just raided their house in South Philadelphia and arrested them. The police were looking to indict others for the same crime. When I saw that, I was so relieved that I gave my mom a big hug, a kiss, and twenty dollars as an offering for her Indian statue. I thought it was the Indian who was protecting me, not knowing that it was Almighty God in heaven who had shown mercy on my soul. From that day on, I went back to my old routine; there was no need to worry about that problem anymore.

Hatred for Christians

Back on the job, Cozzy was still trying to talk to me about Jesus. He didn't tell me his testimony; all he talked about was what Jesus could do for me. This made me so angry; I started hating him.

I had a new car, and Cozzy had an older one. One day as we were going home, I had a seven-millimeter rifle that belonged to an Irish guy named Bill who worked with me. I asked Bill to lend me his rifle and tell everyone it had been stolen. I was going to use it to shoot these Christian guys. They got on my nerves; they preached to me daily. I told Bill that I was going to kill Cozzy on his way home in a drive-by shooting. He took Woodhaven Road to 1-95 South because he lived in South Philadelphia and was the one who closed down the warehouse.

Cozzy was shocked to still see me in the parking lot when he came out of the warehouse. As he got in his car, it started right away, but mine wouldn't start at all. It was a new car, but it took almost fifteen minutes to start. Benny saw me and came to help. When he did, the car started just fine. Today, I know God delivered Cozzy. The Bible says,

"If God is for you, who can be against you?" I didn't know that. God *was* with Cozzy, and not even Joey could come against him. I wasn't able to kill him.

Two weeks later I was working in the warehouse on a forklift truck; I had to pick up skids, each holding four drums of calipers. There were between twenty and thirty skids. John Gallashore was doing the same thing as Cozzy, always trying to preach to me. As I looked at John, I felt so much anger in my heart toward him that I wanted to kill him. I figured I could make it look like an accident if I threw the calipers at him.

I tried to jerk the forklift so that the drums would fall when John was right in front of me; each drum weighed a thousand pounds. Four thousands pounds would fall on John. Instead of falling forward on John, the drums fell backward toward me. They didn't crush me because I jumped off the forklift truck as soon as I noticed what was happening. The drums bent the forklift.

God was also with John Gallashore, and I couldn't come against him either. I hated both of those men because they persisted in preaching Jesus to me. To me, these naïve, dumb Christians looked like squares. I kept telling them that they didn't know what was going on and that they were into nothing. I didn't realize that *I* was the one who was into nothing and that *I* needed to get into what they had.

These men faithfully demonstrated God's love toward me. Each morning they bought me coffee and doughnuts. Sometimes Benny Holland's wife baked a cake, and Benny would bring part of it to work. He tried to share with everyone, but I rejected him. During lunch, Bob, Bill, and I would go outside and mock the Christians. We would laugh at them and call them a bunch of phonies and squares. By buying me coffee and doughnuts, they made me hate them, especially Cozzy and John Gallashore, even more.

Chapter 13

Carmen

At this time in my life, I had no intention of settling down or marrying. I was afraid of entering into a serious relationship because I thought I would probably kill the girl if she put me under pressure by nagging me. However, I always had a lot of girlfriends. I used them for my own benefits and then let them go. Sometimes a girl wanted to be my girlfriend because of the reputation I had; she figured that she would get respect from the other guys. And sometimes girls just wanted to go out with me because they wanted to get back at another guy or wanted me to hurt someone. I was getting really tired of hurting people.

My baby sister, Wandy, attended school at Torresdale and Wakeling Streets in northeast Philadelphia. My sister met the school secretary, who used to catch the bus home with her and they became good friends. The secretary was about twenty-years-old, and I was twenty-one at the time. Wandy could have asked me for anything, and I would have given it to her. I told her that I would buy her a car when she turned sixteen if she did well in school. I bought her and my brother Willie stereos for their rooms. I was making so much money from selling that I could buy them anything they wanted.

It seemed that every time I came home from work Wandy was talking on the phone with her friend. I used to ask her, "Wandy, who are you talking to?" She would answer that it was her friend, the school secretary.

One day I was hurt on the job, so I was home for about two weeks. The buses weren't running due to a strike, so Wandy had asked me to pick her up from school. During the two weeks I was at home, I picked her up every day. I loved my sister Wandy; she was a pretty girl with beautiful brown skin and jet black hair. She and Willie stayed to themselves, playing and fighting with each other. I didn't want Willie to grow up like me and live the same miserable life; I didn't want Wandy to grow up and live the way my other sisters lived.

My other sisters left home and lived with their boyfriends. Vivian was the only one who was married. I was trying to keep Wandy from going down that same route. Whenever she asked me for something, I would go out of my way for her and for Willie.

On the third day that I was home from work, I went to pick Wandy up at school, and she invited her friend to come too. Her friend's name was Carmen. When I pulled up to get my sister, she asked if I could also take Carmen home. I said yes. Wandy jumped in the front, and Carmen and another girl got in the back. I talked with Carmen and tried to be nice to her. Carmen lived at the corner of Fifth and Clearfield Streets.

I remembered walking through that neighborhood and seeing her and her sister looking out the window. I asked Carmen if she came from a very strict family; she asked me why I wanted to know, and then she told me that her parents were strict. I related the scene of walking through her neighborhood and seeing her looking out the window. It seemed to me that she never left her house, but she said she did come out to go to parties every now and then.

"I just don't like to go out that much," she commented. Carmen was very pretty and had a beautiful smile. I thought to myself, "Wow, Wandy has a nice-looking friend!" She was also friendly and sociable.

We finally arrived at her house, and I told her that I would be picking Wandy up from school every day and could pick her up too if she needed a ride home.

"Yes," she replied, "I'd appreciate that."

The next day, I went to school to pick up Wandy and her friend. I did this just to be nice to her; there was still some good in me. If you were my friend and didn't have any money, I would give you some. If you didn't have a coat, I would give you mine. But if you did me wrong, I would blow you away the next day. That's the type of person I was. I kept myself distant from everyone; I never told other people what was in my heart.

Carmen and I would talk after I picked up her and Wandy. However, I had no intention of dating her or getting close to her. I was living the fast life.

After I dropped off Wandy and Carmen, I would go pick up another girl, get high, or sell drugs. Occasionally, I wouldn't come home at all because I stayed the night at some girl's house. I went home early in the morning, just long enough to take a shower before I went to work; that was the kind of life I lived.

When I went back to work, Wandy told me that her friend was asking a number of questions about me. My sister often came to me, asking some very personal questions. Finally, I confronted Wandy, "Why are you asking me so many questions about my personal life?" She didn't want to tell me that her friend was trying to find out about me! Wandy asked me if I had a girlfriend, and I told her that I didn't. Soon I became so tired of her asking me these questions that I told her I had a lot of girlfriends.

My sister replied, "No, Joey, you can only have one, and a good woman at that." I looked at Wandy and smiled because I could see she was growing up.

Does She Know Who I Am?

Wandy greeted me one day as I came in from the streets, saying her friend wanted to talk to me. I asked my sister, "Talk to me about what? I haven't seen her in almost two months." Wandy told me that Carmen wanted me to call her. I was surprised and asked Wandy, "Does your friend know who I am?" I knew that Wandy's friend wouldn't want

110

anything to do with me if she were aware that I was a criminal known in our neighborhood as King. Carmen appeared to be a decent young lady, and she wasn't living the kind of life I lived.

My sister called her and talked with her for awhile. Wandy waited for me to go into the kitchen, and then she told Carmen I wanted to talk to her. Wandy was playing matchmaker, trying to get us together. Wandy passed the phone to me, and I started to talk to her friend. I asked her what she wanted and why she wanted to talk with me; she asked what I meant by that. I answered, "Wandy said you wanted to talk to me."

Carmen was surprised to hear that, but her voice told me she was also pleased. She repeated what Wandy had conveyed to her. Then we both realized what Wandy was trying to do. Since we were already on the phone and she was a nice looking girl, I asked if I could talk to her. I wanted to get to know her better if it was all right with her. Carmen said she didn't mind.

We became friends, and I would call her up two or three times a week with no intention of becoming her boyfriend. I kept saying to myself, "If this girl finds out who I am, she won't want anything to do with me."

At one point, I was laid-off from Cardo's for thirty days. I didn't care; I was selling drugs and wouldn't really lose anything. Because Wandy got out of school at 2:00 p.m., I could pick up her and Carmen. One day I told Carmen I would like to take her out on a date, and she replied that it was fine with her.

Carmen was not only beautiful, but she possessed a sweet and gentle personality. She told me I couldn't come to her house yet; she wanted to get to know me better before I met her family. I comforted myself with the thought that I had no intention of going to her house. If no one knew I was seeing her, then no one could tell her I was messing around with other girls.

After getting to know her better, I found out she had never been with anyone before. I looked at this as an opportunity to be the first one to become intimate with her. I always kept myself well dressed, wearing expensive shoes, gold watches, and diamond rings. Carmen thought the reason I always looked nice was that I had a job. She didn't know anything about my past life or my drug business. I saw how sweet she was, but my real intention was to get over on her. I thought she would be an easy girl to do that to; but she wasn't. Once when we went out on a date and sat in the car, I started to kiss and touch her. She grabbed both my hands and kept them away from her. That really impressed me because every other girl I knew was fast. I thought that she might be a bit more difficult but that some day she would give in.

Wandy was happy because Carmen and I were dating, but the less we were seen together, the better it was for me. I didn't want to tell Carmen about my past life. I knew that if I told her how I lived and what I had done, she would become scared and leave me. I was trying my best to keep everything undercover. I dated Carmen for about six months, yet no one from my neighborhood or any of my friends knew about it. The only person who knew everything was Richie because he and I were always together.

Carmen and I would spend a few hours together; then I would drop her off around the corner from her house. I would go home, take a shower, and go back out on the streets to my fast lifestyle: getting high, selling drugs, and running around with other women. The thought occurred to me that I might want to marry a woman like Carmen some day, but I knew I couldn't be faithful to anyone.

Wandy continued to talk constantly about Carmen. When I didn't want to see her, I would call her and tell her I was going to stay in for the rest of the day; that was a lie. I always ended up getting high with the guys.

On the weekends when she would call me, she would never find me at home. We saw each other two or three days a week and I liked that because I wanted to keep what I had in the streets. I didn't know if I was ready to settle down. At times, I thought that she might be the woman of my dreams and that maybe she could help me get out of the mess I was in and live the good life I wanted. I really wanted a life of peace; I wanted to have children and be a good father to them. I didn't want to treat them as my father had treated me.

Deep in my heart I never knew what it was to really love someone. I never loved any girl I had as a girlfriend. To me, love was only pleasure and a way to satisfy my needs as a man. I didn't know what it was to love a woman, and I was afraid that if I ever became serious with anyone, I might kill her if she made me angry.

After dating Carmen for six months, I figured it would be best to stay away from her. Many on-going battles filled my life. I couldn't sleep at night, and my sins continued to torment me. I was high every time I went to work. I didn't know what to do about Carmen; should I stay with her or let her go? "Am I really ready for this?" I would ask myself. I knew that if I seduced Carmen and let her go, Wandy would be terribly hurt. I loved Wandy so much that I didn't want to hurt her, so I decided I would stay away from Carmen.

Telling the Truth

The visits and the phone calls slowed down, and Carmen realized I wasn't trying to see her as often. Even though I started this relationship with the thought of using her for my pleasure, my motives changed because I saw the kind of girl she was. I really wanted her to be happy. I didn't want her to live the kind of life the women I knew were living. They were always miserable. Some of them killed themselves because they thought there was nothing to live for.

Finally, I decided to tell Carmen everything about my past. She met me at Bridge and Pratt Streets, and we went to a park on Susquehanna and Howard Streets — Diamond Square Park. While we sat in the car, I began to relate a story about a guy that I knew. As I told the story, she didn't realize that I was telling her about myself.

Carmen asked me what the guy's name was, and I told her it was "Joe." I told her that when this guy was a kid, he was already a criminal, in and out of juvenile homes, in and out of prison. He lived in the streets, and sometimes he ran away from home. His mother had to put food in a pot and leave it in the backyard for him to eat. Often the food wasn't covered and flies would get into it, but he would have to eat it anyway.

She responded sympathetically, "Wow! You know people who have lived that kind of life?"

I continued, "This guy lived a lonely and miserable life, but people liked to have him around. No one really knew what Joe was going through. He lived the fast life, starting when he was young. He shot and stabbed people and even had a reputation of being a rapist. Some of the stories people told about him were true, but much of it was a lie."

Carmen kept asking me the same question: "Do you really know people like that?"

I told her that this guy, Joe, was the leader of one of the biggest gangs in Philadelphia and that he was a notorious criminal. He stole money from many people and ran around with quite a few women. Joe felt as if he could never settle down.

"He sounds," she said, "like a very lonely man. Someone like that has to be miserable."

"Believe me," I told her, "he's *really* miserable." I told her Joe had a job and was a hard worker. Even though he was a drug dealer, he was trying to get out of that world and become a good person who would contribute to society. However, he felt his past followed him.

114

Carmen told me, "We can't judge a book by its cover." I replied that she was absolutely right, but unfortunately, people often judge others by what they see on the outside. She responded, "You can't condemn a person for his past because people change."

I agreed. I knew people who *had* changed and asked her if she really believed people could change. Carmen said yes and told me that she and her whole family were in church; she had grown up in the things of God.

I asked her, "Do you think there's hope for Joe?"

"Of course, there's hope for Joe," she replied. I reinforced the fact that this man had done so many bad things, but she continued to tell me there was hope for Joe.

Then I told her the truth. "I *am* Joe."

Carmen was sitting right next to me, but when she heard that, she moved over. She looked into my eyes, and I told her, "Look, I am going to tell you something. Everything I have told you about Joe is really about me. I just wanted to be honest with you." My feelings for Carmen had become serious, and I was sorry I had lied to her. I admitted, "You don't really want me, and there's no hope for me. No one can change me. Nothing can change a man who has shed so much blood and hurt so many people. I have scars in my heart no one can heal. I have been called a career criminal, and I will always be one. Since I've been with you, all I have been doing is running around." Although that had been true at the beginning of our relationship, for the past two months I had been so involved with her that I hadn't slept with another woman. I was even trying to stay away from the gangs and drugs.

I had hoped she would be the girl who could help me change my life. Being truthful, I confessed that I had stopped calling and seeing her because I was running with other women. I didn't want to hurt her feelings, but I also didn't want her to fall in love with me and later find out about my past. I informed her that she could walk out of this

115

relationship. I told her that if she stayed with me, all I would want to do was get over on her because she was a virgin, and I didn't care about her.

That last part was a lie. I said those things because I was afraid to enter into a more serious relationship with her, knowing I could never be faithful to her. I felt even if we went so far as to get married, I would start doing my own thing again within six months — running around with other women and selling drugs.

When Carmen looked at me, I saw tears in her eyes, and she said to me, "I would never have imagined you were that type of guy."

I told her, "This is who I am. I don't enjoy telling people what I have done, but everything I have told you is true. There is no changing that now. Carmen, I don't want to hurt you. You are an intelligent and beautiful young woman. Find someone better than me because I'm no good for you." I was speaking to her from the deepest part of my heart. I had never opened up so much to anyone in my life, even to Richie.

Carmen looked at me and drew close again, saying, "Joey, I love you. Do you think you can change?"

I told her nothing could change me. I also confided that I was falling in love with her, which was the reason I had to be honest; I did not want to hurt her.

"Joey," she encouraged, "I know people who used to live the kind of life you have described, and they have changed. If you want, I'll try to help you."

I wanted to break down crying when she said that, but I couldn't because I always kept my tears in my heart. I stared at her and said, "You help me? No one can help me."

"Joey, that's what's wrong with you. You're always thinking negatively. I've been studying you for the past six months, and you have such a low image of yourself. You can change, Joey. If you want, I'll help you, but you have to do your part."

I didn't say anything. I just started the car and drove her home. She asked if she could see me again.

"Yes, I'll call you. My sister Wandy really loves you and thinks the world of you. I would never do anything to hurt you or Wandy." Smiling, she hugged me, got out of the car, and walked away.

Chapter 14

A Change of Heart

I drove home, took a shower, and went by myself to the Art Museum at Fairmount Park. Parking the car, I got out and walked to the museum. I had some marijuana and two quarts of beer. As I sat there by myself, smoking marijuana and drinking beer, I pondered what Carmen had said to me earlier — that I could change, that there was a way to change.

She didn't know that by saying that to me she was causing me to fall more and more in love with her. That night she called me; we talked for awhile, and Carmen asked me if everything was okay. For the next week, I stayed at home. All the gang members and the guys who used to hang out in the bar wondered what had happened to me. I was trying to get away from them to see if I really could change.

"Maybe Carmen has something that could help me," I wondered. Back then, that was the only week I experienced peace in my life. My mind was blank, and I didn't think about the past. I stayed at home all week because I wanted to think things over. Did I really want to change? Did I want to get serious with this girl? I liked the fast life, the easy money, the fast women, and the reputation I had. During that week, I only talked to Carmen on the phone; I didn't get to see her. After the week was over, I met with her, and she asked me why I was staying home so much.

"Look," I told her, "I want you to be my girlfriend as of today." Now the relationship was really beginning to be serious. I still hung out with the guys, but my heart wasn't in it anymore; my heart was with Carmen. When I went out, women still threw themselves at me, but I couldn't see myself taking advantage of the opportunity. I kept thinking about Carmen and the love she had for me, which had given me hope. We continued this way for two or three months.

What is Love?

My foreman, Cozzy, began to see a change in me. One day on my break I was writing a poem. Cozzy came over to me. "Hey, Joe, what's that you're writing?"

Even though I thought I hated him, my heart was starting to soften due to the talk I'd had with Carmen. I told him it was a poem. He asked me if I was in love or something, and I warned him to mind his own business! There was something about Cozzy that drew me to him even though I didn't want to admit it. Cozzy was like a father. He always tried to talk to me, and he looked me in the eye — something my father never did. I never knew the color of my father's eyes. Cozzy found ways to get to me. He was constantly throwing a little "Gospel seed" into my heart. Cozzy asked me if he could read my poem, and I said yes.

When Cozzy read the poem, his response inspired hope in me. "Joe, do you see the talent you have? You're letting it go to waste!"

"What do you mean?" I asked. "It's a piece of paper; it's worthless."

"It's from your heart, Joe. If you give the girl this poem, she's going to fall in love with you even more. Joe, when you get it typed up; would you give me a copy so that I can give it to my wife?"

Again I said yes.

It was the first time in my life that I felt someone appreciated what I had done. I took the poem home. My sister Vivian typed it, and I put Carmen's picture on it. It was really nice because she looked like an angel in the picture. I gave Cozzy a copy of it. He had everyone at work reading it, and they all wanted a copy of it too. I really felt important, not realizing that my heart was softening. Beginning that day, Cozzy started to tell me about himself.

After framing the poem and the picture, I called Carmen to tell her that I wanted to meet her and that I had a little something I wanted to give her. I had always thought gold, silver, and other material things were what impressed women because those things were all I knew. I wrapped it up, and I gave it to her. When she finally got it open, she read the poem and looked at me. I could see in her eyes that she received this with more joy than any of the gold jewelry I had given her. She was really excited about the poem, and I asked her why. After all, it was only a piece of paper! She planted several kisses and a really big hug on me. I finally pushed her away and asked, "What's wrong with you? It's just a piece of paper! You act as if I gave you million dollars."

She replied, "This might only be a piece of paper, but what you have on it is from your heart; it shows that there is good in your heart, Joey. Look at the talent you have, and you don't even know it. There's so much good in you, Joey. You might have done bad things in the past, but there is still something good inside you. This means more to me than any piece of gold you have given me because this is from your heart. This is a piece of *you*."

I was confused, and I didn't know what to say. I didn't know what to think! I asked myself, "Am I really falling in love? What is love?" I didn't know what love was. I thought love was having sex, but now everything was different. Whenever I took her home and returned to my house, the peace I felt when I was around Carmen left me. She always spoke positive things into my life, and even though she wasn't a Christian, she had received a Christian upbringing.

Change was apparent in my life, but I still was afraid to go to sleep. My past tormented me, and I kept having horrible nightmares about people killing me.

A Seed of Life

Cozzy pulled me to the side one day and said, "Joe, I need to talk to you." I was so frustrated, burdened, and confused that I didn't want to talk to anyone. I was getting less and less sleep at night. I also knew my feelings were growing deeper toward Carmen, and sooner or later I would have to meet her family. They were going to reject me; I just knew it. I once had a girlfriend named Cindy whose family did the same thing to me, and the pain was still there.

As Cozzy called me over, I told him, "I don't need to talk to you. Just get out of my face, okay?"

"Joe, you don't have any peace. For the past two weeks I have watched you come in every morning, and your eyes have dark circles all around them. You're not getting enough sleep. Joe, you're putting out good work, but you're losing weight. I can see this. You don't have peace. Joe, listen to me for once! Jesus Christ is the solution to your problems."

When I heard that, I replied angrily, "Listen, I don't want to hear anything about Jesus. I don't believe in God. I don't believe in the devil. You think that because I sat with you the other day, let you read my poem, and gave you a copy of it, we're friends? Well, I don't like you. I don't like white people. I don't like black people, and I don't even like Puerto Ricans because I hate everyone."

In my heart I didn't mean what I said. Something was happening inside me, and I didn't know what was going on. I knew I had offended Cozzy, but I also knew I didn't want to offend him because I was beginning to really like him. I saw a father image in Cozzy, and I even liked to hear what he had to say about Jesus Christ.

Cozzy said, "Joe, I want to show you something."

He took off his shirt, and when he did that, I thought he wanted to fight! I told him I would be right back. I went to the car and got a gun. I can't explain the mixed emotions I

121

was feeling; I was angry, and yet I wasn't. There was a battle going on inside of me. I told Cozzy that if he wanted to fight I would fight him. I knew he didn't want to do that; all he wanted me to do was listen to him. He wanted to tell me something very important to him, and he also wanted to show me something.

I had the gun in my hand when Cozzy said, "No, Joe, I don't want to fight you. I just want to show you this." When he took off his T-shirt, I saw the scars on his body from bullet holes and stab wounds. He pulled down his pants and showed me bullet scars on his legs. He had received five bullet wounds and seven stab wounds in his body.

"Joe," he explained, "I wasn't raised in church. I haven't been a Christian all my life. It's been only four years since I asked Jesus to come into my heart."

I interrupted, "Man, where have you been? In Vietnam? What happened to you?"

Cozzy continued, "Joe, when I was a little boy, I was baptized into the mob. From an early age, I was a juvenile delinquent. I have been a convict, and I used to traffic drugs from state to state. When I was a little boy, I had quite a reputation. I haven't been in the church all my life. I've been in government programs, and I've been a fugitive from the law."

He said, "I used to go to the houses of people who owed the mob money. I would break their legs and tie them up in the basement. We'd take their furniture, their jewelry, and anything else to pay back the debts they owed to the mob. I lived a miserable life. I shed blood and committed violent crimes. I used to treat my wife like she was a dog because I didn't know how to treat a woman. I didn't know how to treat anyone. Joe, my family never loved me. I was considered a problem to society. I was continually afraid that people were going to shoot me or stab me."

As he told me this, I gazed into his eyes, and he was looking straight at me. Each time he spoke, I stared at him because he didn't appear to be the type of a man he was describing. "You don't look like a criminal." All the time he spoke, I could see my life reflected in his. Everything he had gone through, I was going through now. I feared someone was going to shoot me or stab me.

He continued, "Joe, I didn't have peace. I was always running, thinking that someone was going to kill me. Joe, four years ago in a bar, I fell on my knees. I called on God, and He answered me. I said, 'God, I am a sinner. I'll do whatever You want; just change my life.' When I called on God, He answered me, and I felt a burden was lifted from me. I felt as if electricity were running through my body. It was the blood of Jesus cleansing me from all my sins. Starting that day, I felt brand new. From that time, I have had peace in my life. For the last four years, Joe, and to this day, I have loved Jesus. He wants to do the same thing in your life."

When Cozzy said that, he was getting through to me, but there was a battle going on inside. I wanted to do what was right, but I couldn't. I wanted to change, but I couldn't. Then I began to yell at Cozzy, as if all the anger in my heart was coming to the surface. "God ain't real. If God is real, why did He let you get shot and stabbed? I've shot people and stabbed them too. I've hurt many people. I've been in and out of prison and juvenile homes and have never been shot or stabbed, and God is not with *me*."

Cozzy replied, "Joe, if you have done everything you say you did, and you were never shot or stabbed, it is because God has a plan for your life. That's why He brought you here to this factory — to save you, Joe. The owners of this company are Christians, and about three hundred employees in the main building are Christians too."

"Why would God put you in a Christian environment if He didn't want to save you? We pray in this company every day, Joe. In this warehouse, you know that out of twenty-five of us twelve are Christians. Every day we pray for you, Joe. Do you think it is a coincidence that you're here? No, it's God's divine purpose. He wants you to hear these stories. God wants you to hear what I'm sharing with you, because He wants to set you free."

"Maybe God has placed this girl, Carmen, in your path. She may not be a Christian, but she may be there to help you, Joe."

I continued to yell at Cozzy because I didn't want to hear what he had to say. "No one can change me! There isn't anyone who can do that! I don't even want to hear about God. Don't even talk to me about Him anymore. God can't change me," and I walked away.

As I did, Cozzy called out to me again and said, "Joe, Jesus Christ loves you! I have already planted a *seed* in your heart."

I looked at him and laughed. Taking what he had said as a joke, I asked, "What are you going to sow, a marijuana seed?"

He had an answer for me. "No, I'm planting a seed of *life*!"

When he said that, it was as if a spear came out of his mouth and entered right into my heart. Suddenly, I felt a peace I had never felt before.

Chapter 15

God Is Calling!

While working, I thought about Carmen and her family; one day I would have to meet them. No matter how much I changed on my own, they were going to reject me. They would never forgive my past. I began to think I should cut her loose and forget about her. Suddenly, a thought came to my mind. It spoke in a very soft voice, but it tormented me. "Joey, kill yourself." I began to dwell upon that thought, saying to myself, "Maybe that's what I need to do. Maybe if I kill myself, I'll find some peace. There would be one less criminal the law and society would have to deal with."

Then I heard another voice in my mind. It was also very calm and quiet, saying, "Joey, a lot of people want to see you dead. Don't just kill yourself; take some other people with you." That sounded good to me, and I decided that's what I would do. On my break time I began to make a list. The first person on the list was my father. I blamed my parents for the life I lived. After my father, I was going to kill my brother Philip because he was holding up my drug dealers and messing up my business. After Philip, I would kill my mother because I knew she would suffer over Philip's death. She already suffered so much because Mikey was dead, and because she blamed me for it, I would kill her too. Even though I loved my father, mother, and Philip, I think I hated them even more.

After my father, Philip, and my mother, I had the names of four of my drug dealers — Izzy, Georgie, Kiki, and Junior — because they were all messing up with my drug money. After them, I was going to go to the Italian guys in South Philly and tell them to give me the forty thousand dollar contract to kill those four people they wanted dead. I was going to give the money to my younger sisters and brothers. Then I planned to kill my girlfriend Carmen and her parents. I had sent some flowers to her mother on Mother's Day to see if she would receive me, not for what I was but for what I was trying to become. She threw them out the window into the trash. That broke my spirit even more.

I had seventeen people on the list.

Suddenly, I began to cry, and I couldn't understand why. It was as if someone had taken a key, put it in my heart, and opened it up. I was crying and shaking. I already had a great deal of pain in my stomach, possibly due to ulcers from constantly worrying about my problems. However, as I was crying, those tears came from the deepest part of me. Tears were running down my face, and my body was shaking. I couldn't understand what was happening to me.

The twelve Christians in the warehouse had the key. In the Bible, Jesus told us He has given us the key to heaven, and whatever we bind on earth will be bound in heaven. Whatever we loose on earth will be loosed in heaven. Those Christians had the key, which was prayer. They prayed every day. Even with all the aggravation and hell I was putting them through and all the trouble I had gotten them into, they still kept praying for me.

As I cried and thought about killing all these people, I said to myself, "Why can't I be a normal human being? Why can't I have peace in my heart? Why can't I be a normal person, not filled with violence and always thinking about harming people? Why do I think about shooting and hurting people? Why can't I treat my girlfriend right?" I constantly talked down to Carmen, raising my voice at her and cursing her because of my anger and the sin in my heart. "Why can't I talk to her lovingly and feel the same love for her that she feels for me? Why can't I have the same patience with her that she has with me?"

At that moment, I heard another voice; it was not the voice of a human being. This one was loud, and it reverberated like thunder. It called me from above, just as the Bible says — like a river of rushing waters. The voice sounded as if someone were yelling through a big, hollow pipe. It called me by my name, and the first time I heard it my body began to shake and tremble. It said, "*Jose!*"

My body trembled even more. I felt as if something had been shot into my body. I turned around and asked the guys behind me if they had called me. John Gallashore answered me, saying, "No, we didn't call you."

I continued to cry, and suddenly, I heard the voice a second time. It said, "*José!*" This time it was much louder; my body shook even more. I wiped the tears from my face, looking at John and Juan to see if they had called me again.

They said no. I told them that someone was calling me. I went to Cozzy's office at the front. When I got there, he asked me what was wrong; he must have noticed I was crying. I asked him if he had called me, and he said no. I told him someone had called me twice. He said only half jokingly, "Joe, maybe the Lord is calling you."

I told him I didn't believe in God; God was *not* calling me.

"Joe, God *is* calling you. He has a purpose and a plan for your life, and I believe God is going to use you for His glory."

I went to my work area, grabbed a metal pipe, and put it beside me. I thought to myself, "These Christian guys think I'm playing games with them. If they call me a third time, I'm going to bust them upside their heads with this pipe."

For the next half-hour, nothing happened. I kept looking back to see what the guys around me were doing, not knowing it was God who was calling me. I didn't understand what was taking place. Suddenly, I started crying again. I was thinking about all the pain in my heart, all the rejection I felt, the seventeen people I was planning to kill, and the idea of taking my life right along with them. And I kept on crying.

When I looked in front of me, the wall, which was made out of cinder blocks, had become a giant screen! I felt electricity running through my body, and a cloud covered me. Looking around, all I could see was the thick cloud; my body started to tremble. It is hard to express what happened to me that day, but this is the best way to explain it. I heard that same voice a third time, but now it was much louder; my body jerked and trembled even more. It said, *"JOSE!"*

All I could see before me was a screen similar to the ones in movie theaters. A man behind me started to speak. As he spoke, my body continued to tremble. He called me again by my name and said, "Jose, why didn't they shoot you this day?" He showed me all the times I had encountered death. He showed me the day I was gang warring with the guys from Fifth and Westmoreland, and they never shot the pistol or the rifle they had with them.

He showed me when I was twelve and running from the police. I jumped from a three-story building and broke both my legs. Although I never went to the hospital, six months later, I was walking normally again. Next on the screen, I saw myself chained by my neck in the basement of my house, and I heard myself saying, "I'm going to kill my father. I'm going to kill my father." It was revealed to me when I had opened the doors of darkness and allowed it to come into my heart, possessing my life. I saw myself as a little boy rejected by my mother, my father, and society. When I was only twelve, people in my community called me a child of the devil. The man showed me being stabbed seventeen times in front of Church's Chicken on Orianna and Lehigh while fighting nine guys. My gang members pulled my leather coat off to examine me. The coat was all cut up, but the knives never touched my flesh.

He displayed the time I was in the discotheque, and twenty guys were ready to kill me as I yelled, "Kill me! Kill me!" For some reason, they never touched me. I watched myself as I drove my brand new car through a window and down into a basement at Sixteenth and Wallace Streets when I was nineteen. The tires were all blown out, but nothing happened to me; I came out without a scratch. He showed me when I went before a judge at the age of twelve or all the violent crimes I had committed, and the judge said to me, "I don't know why, but I have to let you go." Next, I was in the government program facing ten to twenty years, but I never had to do the time. I saw all the times I was in jail and all the crimes I had committed, receiving only probation for most of them.

He showed me that He had a plan for my life.

The man spoke to me for about an hour, and the more he spoke, the more I wept. I wanted to look back to see who was speaking to me, but I couldn't. I called out, "Who are you? Who are you?" However, I wasn't able to see who he was.

Suddenly, I felt as if something lifted off me. I no longer felt the sensation of electricity in my body anymore. I felt very sick to my stomach and began to vomit. As I threw up, Cozzy walked by and came over to me, saying, "You don't look good at all!" I told him I was feeling extremely sick to my stomach and wanted to leave work. He sent me home saying, "If you can, try to be here tomorrow." I drove all the way home feeling sick, throwing up again out the car window. I had to stop twice.

Izzy

When I finally reached home, I walked through the door, and my mother was lying on the sofa. She was laid off from work. "Wow! What's wrong with you?" she exclaimed. My eyes were bloodshot and puffed up from crying. My mother continued, "You don't look good at all. You haven't been eating right lately either. You're losing a lot of weight."

"Mom, sit down and listen," I said. I didn't know where to begin, and I didn't know if I should tell anyone what I had seen. People would probably think I was crazy. I told my mother something strange had happened to me at my job, and she asked me about it. "Mom, today for no reason I got this thought in my mind about killing a lot of people. I am tired of life, and I don't know if I want to continue living anymore. As I was working, the thought came to me to kill myself and to take a lot of people with me."

She jumped up and said, "Boy, what do you want to do that for?"

"I heard a voice telling me if I killed all these people and myself, I would find peace at last. I was really thinking about doing it when something strange happened. When I heard the first voice, there was no peace at all. I felt tormented by that voice. I said to myself, 'That's what I'm going to do. I'm going to kill myself and a whole lot of people.' " I told my mother I had made a list of seventeen people I planned to kill. My mother started crying. "Mom, you know how I am when I set my heart to do something," I shrugged.

I continued, "While I was thinking that way, I started to cry. As I was crying, I heard a voice call me, but it wasn't the first voice that tormented me. This voice thundered, and it called me by my name three times. With the third call, I was shown my entire life."

Upon hearing this, my mother stopped crying and started to listen more carefully. She shivered and said, "Boy, you're making the hair on my head stand up!"

I replied, "Mom, this voice displayed a big movie screen on which I saw myself when I was a little boy. I watched when you and Pop rejected me and when Pop chained me up by my neck. It showed me my entire life and why I was never shot or stabbed or killed. It even revealed all the times I was in prison, in the government program, and in mental hospitals.

"It showed me when I was in front of the judge but never went to jail to do hard time for the things I did." All of a sudden, my mother stopped me.

She was really excited as she jumped off the sofa and shouted, "It's the spirit of the Indian; it's the spirit of the Indian! Keep lighting candles to him!"

I shouted, "You're crazy! I don't believe in that stuff. It wasn't an Indian who called me. It was someone else, probably God!"

"Joey, I think you're losing your mind," she said. "I was talking to Gigi's psychiatrist, and he said he wants to see you. I've been telling him all the things you're doing, that you can't sleep at night, and that sometimes you even talk in your sleep about killing people. I told the psychiatrist that you need some help."

I told my mother I didn't believe in the psychiatrist either! She told me every day she lit candles to the Indian, believing that something good was going to come from my life. Then she began to cry again. "Joey, sometimes I look in the room to see if you and Mikey are there. There are times when I wait for someone to knock on the door to tell me that you have been killed. I live in fear of this terrible news."

I was enraged with her after she spoke. I felt like spitting at her and putting a knife through her chest. "I'm getting outta here! You're crazy! You're always lighting candles to those Indians. I know you pray to them and give them money. Sometimes you've almost convinced me. I give the Indians money. I put it in the water you call holy water, and when I come back at night, the money is gone. I know the Indians didn't take it. Someone else is taking the money, so leave me alone about the Indians!"

I got a gun and made up my mind to kill one of my drug dealers who had been failing me for a long time. He owed me about eight hundred dollars in drugs. Instead of giving me the money, he was shooting it all up.

Driving to Fourth and Indiana Streets, I found two girls I knew, Chunky and Little Woman. I saw them walking down the street and gave them a ride. They asked me what I had for them to get high on. I gave them some amphetamines and some marijuana. They asked me if I wanted to go to a party Thursday night. I told them I had to take care of some business first. I wanted to talk to Izzy, whom we also called Big Bird. Izzy was originally from New York, but he had moved to Philadelphia. He was a big guy, tall with a wild-looking hairdo. Even though I really liked him, I was at the point of wanting to kill him because of all the money he owed me. I truly believed that if I didn't kill Izzy everyone else would try to take advantage of me in my drug business.

Arriving at our destination, the two girls got out, walked into the bar, got something to drink, and came back out. When they came out, I was talking with Izzy. Suddenly, I pulled out my gun. Izzy was with a guy named Gun, a black brother named Tom who lived down the street, and two other guys from the gang. I had the gun in my right hand and questioned Izzy, "Where is my money? I'm tired of you playing games with me. I want my money now! I don't care what you have to do to get it, but I want it."

I became even angrier at Izzy because he was high. I knew he didn't have my money, but I also knew that if I didn't do something he would continue to play the same game with me. When the girls with me saw the gun, Little Woman yelled out, "Joey, don't do that! Don't kill him!" I told her to shut up, or I would blow her away too. The girls crossed the street to get away from us.

Looking around, I saw people peering out of their windows. The guys across the street were also staring. Several of the guys who used to buy drugs from me were there. Again, I asked Izzy, "Where is my money? *Where is my money?*"

Izzy replied, "Oh, Joey, I shot it all up."

I said to him, "Oh, you shot it all up, huh?"

132

He pleaded, "Yeah! But I'll give it to you tomorrow, man. Just give me another chance." Izzy had just finished doing seven years in prison in New York, and he was trying to con me with jail psychology. He continued, "Joey, are you going to let a few drugs end our relationship?" He had hoped to soften my heart with that, but I told him that I wanted my money; I wanted it now.

"Don't even try to con me with your talk. If you don't give it to me, I'm going to blow you away in front of everyone here." Hearing myself, I realized that it wasn't me talking. My mouth was moving, but I could hear another voice speaking through me. I didn't know what was happening, but I felt my blood boil. I told Izzy, "Since you shot up all my drug money, I'm going to shoot *you* all up." I lifted my gun, poised to shoot him, but someone patted me on my shoulder.

Chapter 16

Black and White Shadows

Convinced the police were right behind me, I pulled my hand back down and thought of throwing the gun under a car; instead, I quickly put it back in my pocket. When I turned to see who was there, to my great surprise I saw. . . a small, elderly woman!

She had a little bag under her left arm and was holding several small pieces of paper. Realizing she was the one who had tapped me on the shoulder, I began to scream at her, "Lady, you're crazy! Don't you see I'm ready to kill this man, and you're interrupting me?" Speaking like this, I felt as if I were possessed by demons.

Even though I had no respect for her, I was not able to look her straight in the eyes. I told her to get out of my face, but instead she calmly said, "Here, young man." She gave me four Christian tracts.

I was astonished! "You mean to tell me that you interrupted me from killing this guy to give me four pieces of paper? What are these anyway?" Her face glowing, she told me that they were tracts, little printed papers that talked about knowing God.

"I have to tell you something, young man! I go to church on Fifth and Somerset Streets, and while I was praying there with a few other church members, God spoke to me! He told me to get up, take some tracts, and come to this corner because there is a young man here He wants to save — and that young man is you!"

I stared at her, laughed devilishly, and responded, "Miss, you mean to tell me that if there really is a God, He came down from heaven, sat in your church, and started to talk to *you*?"

Patiently, she explained, "No, that's not what happened! God spoke *to my heart*, telling me to get up and come to this corner. There is a young man here He is calling, and He wants to save him because He has a plan and a purpose for his life. That young man is you!"

"Lady, you're crazy! You and all your church people are crazy!" I grabbed the tracts and crushed them in my hand. "You see what I just did with these tracts?" I threw the tracts at her, hitting her in the face with them. "I hate you, and I hate all Christians! I'm fed up with this Jesus stuff!"

Frightened by my screaming, she turned around and began to run across the street. Gun watched the entire episode, horrified. He shouted, "Joey, leave her alone! She's a woman of God!"

Responding that I didn't care who she was, I began to chase her across the street yelling, "I hate you! I hate you!"

When she reached the other side of the street, she stopped, turned around, and looked me dead in the face. "Jesus loves you," she proclaimed, and as she spoke those words, I fell backward and began to tremble inside. I couldn't understand what was happening to me.

Again I screamed, "I hate you!"

And again she told me, "Jesus loves you!" Once more, I fell backward; I couldn't even get near her. A third time she spoke that name, "Jesus loves you!" and then she walked away. I became nervous and confused. Going back to the corner, I forgot about killing Izzy! That thought had left my mind, and I was trembling.

Gun noticed I was shaking and asked, "What's wrong with you, Joe?" I told him I didn't know, but when the woman told me Jesus loved me, my body started to tremble. He explained, "Joe, that lady is my neighbor. She is a woman of God; she is a woman of prayer. She is full of the power of God, so leave her alone!"

Could It Be?

Still trembling, I went into the bar and bought some beer. I was there for half an hour but began to feel sick. I told people I would see them the next day and went home.

My mother saw me and told me I didn't look well at all. I told her that nothing was wrong with me and that she should leave me alone. She continued to nag me, telling me I needed to see the psychiatrist. I replied that I didn't need a psychiatrist. There was nothing wrong with me.

I couldn't sleep that night. Tossing and turning, I finally got up, went outside, and sat on the porch. It was about eleven; I smoked a couple of sticks of marijuana, but I was still trembling inside. That voice in my mind kept telling me to kill those seventeen people and myself. It sounded like my own voice, but it tormented me. I went back to my room and took four 25-mg Valiums. I thought they would knock me out, but they didn't help either.

My bed was on the second floor, right next to the window. I stood on my bed and thought about throwing myself out the window, but for some reason I couldn't move. I began to sob, wondering what was wrong with me. I thought to myself, "Could it really be God calling me? Could God really be using these Christians to speak to me? Could God be using the people in the company to speak to me? Maybe their prayers really are working! Maybe God really is calling me." Finally, I was able to get some sleep.

The next morning I got up and went to work, where I called my girlfriend Carmen and told her that I needed to see her. I thought I was losing my mind. I planned to leave work early so that she could meet me at Bridge and Pratt streets; I would pick her up there. We went to Fairmount Park and sat in the car. I shared my problems with her, relating that something very strange had happened to me yesterday.

"Carmen, I don't think people are going to believe me when I tell them what happened. People are going to think I'm crazy, but I know I'm not. I know what happened to me! Yesterday, when I was at work, I thought about killing seventeen people. I was even thinking about killing you and your parents. I thought about killing my own parents, Philip, and several other people."

"I am tired of life, and I have no peace in my heart! I try to be good to you, but I hate the way I treat you. I don't even know why you're still here, but you are; I really appreciate that. You're the only person who has ever given me hope by telling me that I could change."

"Even though I am trying to change, it's hard because my past won't leave me alone. It runs after me day and night. It seems as if I'm always running away from it, but it always catches up with me. Yesterday, while I had those thoughts of killing people, I heard another voice calling me. It was loud, like thunder, and it called me by name. And it called me a second time, but I thought it was the guys who were working behind me. I thought they were playing games with me, and I was going to bust them upside their heads with a pipe if they called me again."

"The voice called me a third time, and I was shown my entire life, as if a large movie screen were placed in front of me. It showed me all the times I wasn't shot, stabbed, or killed. It showed me when I didn't do hard time for the crimes I had committed. I don't know what is happening to me. I don't know to whom this voice belongs. I do know that when it called my name peace came upon me — a peace I have never felt before in my life."

Carmen was amazed, exclaiming, "Wow! You're telling me this, and I'm getting goose bumps. You know, Joey, the Bible talks about God calling men by their names. It could be God calling you."

"I don't want to hear that!" I argued. "God is not real, and the devil is not real!" Of course, the devil kept me from believing he was real. As long as he could do that, he could also keep me from believing there was a solution to my problems. I asked Carmen, "Do you think God could be calling me?"

"Yes," she replied, "Maybe you need to go to church and try God."

"Go to church? If I go to church, the whole building will fall down! No God can forgive me for all the crimes I have committed."

Carmen wouldn't give up. "Yes, Joey, God can forgive you." She began to tell me how Moses killed a man, and God forgave him; Saul (Paul) sent people to their deaths, and God forgave him too, she said. She continued to share Bible stories with me about people who sinned before God and about how He forgave them and used them mightily.

The Battle Continues

Maybe I would go to church one day but not right now. I didn't feel good. I took her to her house, and then I went home. Thinking about all the things she shared from the Bible, I said to myself, "Maybe I *should* go to church."

Friday night I spoke to her; Sunday morning I got up and went to a church to see what was going on. I wanted to see if God was really doing all of this, so I went to St. Peter's Catholic Church on Fifth Street and Girard Avenue. Walking in, I didn't know what to do. After finding the offering box, I placed some change inside, hoping good might come from it; maybe that night I would have peace, I thought. What really caught my attention was the figure of a dead person inside a glass casket. I asked someone who it was, and the person told me the dead person was an important priest from the past. The priest looked as if he were made out of wax.

Kneeling down, I said, "God, if You are real and if You are calling me, then let me know it is You doing this." When I left the church, I still didn't have peace; I went in without peace, and I left the same way.

I stayed home that day until close to five o'clock, and then I went down into the neighborhood to drink with the guys on the corner. I wanted to tell Richie, Gun, and Shake and Bake what was going on, but I only stayed for about ten minutes everywhere I went. Because I thought someone was chasing me, I drifted in and out of different places. I kept looking behind me, thinking that someone was following me to shoot me from behind; I didn't even trust my best friends.

Finally, I decided to go home, but I still couldn't sleep. All I could hear were the voices in my mind telling me I would find peace by killing those seventeen people and myself. This went on all night; I took more Valium, drank several beers, and at last went to sleep. I thought being high and drunk were my only source of peace.

The next morning, I prepared for work and smoked two sticks of marijuana. On the way to work, I picked up my friends, Bill and Bob. We smoked more marijuana, and they talked about all the things they had done over the weekend. I just listened. Arriving early at the factory, we went to buy coffee and doughnuts from a lunch truck. We smoked more marijuana, and Bob and Bill went into the factory. I stayed behind to wrap up the small amount of marijuana I had left.

As I opened the door to go inside, a black shadow went past me. I moved back, wondering, "Wow, what was that?" I didn't pay too much attention to it, thinking it was from lack of sleep or a drug flashback. I punched in my time card and went to my work area. As I worked, I thought about Carmen; I knew we weren't going to last long. Things were not good between us. She was twenty-years-old at the time, and I was almost twenty-two. She was going through a great deal by seeing me because her parents didn't want us together. They really angered me, and I didn't feel like dealing with them.

As I continued to work, I saw the black shadow go by me again, and it started to torment me. It went past and screamed in my ear to kill those people and myself. Over and

139

over it repeated this to me. When the black shadow came near a third time to torment me, a man in a white robe chased after it. His robe shined like a fluorescent light. Peace overwhelmed me as he shot by. I still thought I was having flashbacks from the drugs I took that morning

Then I felt a battle begin in my life. The man in a white robe chasing a black shadow occupied my entire day. The more I saw the black shadow, the less peace I had; the more I saw the man in the white robe shoot by me, the greater the peace that came over me.

I told my foreman I must have eye problems because of all the black and white shadows I was seeing. I informed him I wasn't tripping on anything; I just needed to go to the eye doctor to have it checked out. I made an appointment to go the following afternoon.

The next morning, I went to work, but the battle continued. I didn't understand back then what was taking place, but now I know it was a true spiritual battle for my life.

Chapter 17

The Man in the Cloud

I went to Scheie Eye Institute on Fortieth and Market streets. When I arrived for my appointment, a Chinese doctor saw me. He asked me what problem I was having. I related my story: "For the past two days I have seen a black, tormenting shadow go by me, and then a white shadow chases it away, bringing me great peace."

The doctor checked my eyes and told me there was nothing wrong with them; they looked fine. Then he told me the dark and white shadows I was seeing were "beetles in the air." I told him they didn't look like beetles to me! With that, I left. Some drops had been put into my eyes, making difficult for me to see clearly. Because I couldn't see well enough to drive back to work, I stayed home the rest of the day.

For the next month, this battle continued in my life. I was so tormented by this black shadow that I wrecked my new car. Anger and frustration caused me to try to squeeze the car between a truck and a wall. Not realizing a pole was sticking out of the pavement, I drove into it.

I continued going down to the neighborhood on Fourth and Indiana, keeping a gun on me at all times. Twice, I was ready to open fire on people across the street from me for no apparent reason. I saw them laughing, and I thought they were laughing at me. One of them owed me money, and I thought he was laughing because he was getting over on me.

Some of the guys in the neighborhood liked me and some didn't. Others only wanted me around when they needed me to bail them out of trouble. I had a number of emotional difficulties; I thought everyone was trying to take advantage of me. Every day I went down to the neighborhood with that thought in mind.

I crossed the street to shoot the guy who was laughing. I pulled out my gun, and it seemed as if something left me; I suddenly found myself in my right mind. I thought, "What happened here? What is this gun doing in my hand?" I put it back in my pocket.

The Pressure Increases

Every now and then I would tell Carmen what was going on with me, and she'd ask me if I was going to church. I told her I wasn't. She replied that she would go with me if I wanted. "If there is really a God," I told her, "He's going to have to help me. I don't know what's taking place in my life any longer. If God doesn't help me soon, I am afraid I'm going to kill myself and a lot of other people too."

"Joey, I'll go with you to church on Sunday, and then we can go out from there."

Sunday came, and we went to a Catholic church. The priest spoke in a language I'd never heard before. I didn't feel any peace. I finally told Carmen I wanted to leave. "This is awful! It's baloney!" Once we were outside, I began screaming at her, putting her down and telling her that she was no good and that she should leave me alone. Despite the fact that I insisted I didn't want her anymore, she stayed, hanging in there with me.

After Carmen helped me calm down, we went to a park near Thirty-third and Lehigh Streets. All I wanted to do was cry. I wanted to open up my heart to Carmen and tell her all my problems. I wanted to tell her how I really felt inside; I just wanted to die. There was no reason for me to keep on living. My pain was too great, and my wounds were too deep; I didn't want to live anymore. I could no longer face reality. Sometimes I didn't even want to be near Carmen because she was so clean and innocent. Even though I kept myself clean physically, I felt dirty inside. I often told her to find someone else. She didn't need me, and it would be better if she forgot about me. I felt as if I were a failure; that's what I had heard all of my life. Carmen was the only person who gave me hope.

After sometime, I took her home, and she asked me if I was going to call her the next day. I said I would call her from work. But I didn't call her; I just wanted to be by myself to think about what I was going to do. I knew I couldn't be faithful to her. Each time I was with someone else, I felt dirty because of what I was doing to her. Sometimes, I tried to convince myself that I could continue to live this way, hoping my infidelity would stop when Carmen and I finally married. That was the mentality I had, but even then, it was hard for me to really believe it. I was afraid that if I married her I might kill her because of the way I thought. I had a terrible temper, and I knew how dangerous I could be at times.

Still seeing the shadows, my battle within continued without let-up. Often when driving my car, I would turn around quickly to look behind me; I sensed someone sitting in the back seat. Occasionally, I would go to open the car door, and I would see a shadow standing in front of it. Then I would see it run. The white shadow would appear, and again a tremendous peace would come over my life

At work, I told John what I was going through. I told him that a few months ago I was at work and for no apparent reason I started to cry. "I'm going to tell you something, and you hear me clearly," I said to him. "Listen to what I'm telling you, but don't you preach to me about God because I don't want to hear it. I told you I don't believe in God." I continued to tell him I didn't know why I had cried that day, but it had come from the deepest part in my heart. A thought had come to me about killing several other people and myself. "Ever since then, I've thought about doing just that. But then I heard a voice call me three times by name and show me why I was never shot, stabbed, or killed. Since then, strange things have started happening to me."

As I told this to John, he told me he sensed the presence of God; I told him I didn't want to hear *anything* about God. I went on to say that ever since that time I would see a tormenting black shadow shoot past me, followed by a white shadow, which chased it away. I didn't know if the white shadow was a ghost or not.

Excitedly, John said, "Joe, there is nothing wrong with you! You know, God is showing you what you're going to fight in the future."

"Fight what?" I responded perplexed. "I can't even grab the thing!"

"It is not with your hands that you are going to grab this, Joe," John explained. "It is not with your hands that you are going to fight it. You must be born again. You must accept Jesus Christ as your Lord and Savior. You need to put on the full armor of God and learn from Him, and He will fight the battle for you. He will show you how to fight the devil. What you are seeing is a spiritual battle; God is fighting for your soul, Joe!"

"Shut up! I told you I don't want to hear about God. Didn't I tell you not to preach to me?" I was extremely angry with him and continued, "I came to ask you for some advice, and here you are trying to preach to me!"

"Joe, I am praying for you every day. God showed me that He is calling you. He has a plan for your life."

I told John to get out of my face. "As a matter of fact, the next time you come to tell me about this Jesus or even mention His name I'm going to shoot you right here in this factory."

He told me that Jesus loved me and then walked away. I went back to my work area and started to classify water pumps and clutches. We were the ones who classified all the motor parts, both old and new. That day, some clutches had been delivered from a factory that had gone out of business. I had to remove them from the boxes, sort them,

144

and then put them in Cardo's boxes. Every now and then, Cozzy would walk by me, happy and in good spirits. Cozzy always told me I was doing a good job; he used to say, "I wish I had ten or twenty guys just like you!"

As I started to sort the clutches, I heard those tormenting voices in my mind again. Very softly, they began telling me to kill those people and to do it *today*; if I did, I would find peace. The voices kept repeating themselves like an echo. I tried to reject those thoughts, but they returned still louder. I was also thinking about what John told me concerning God calling me and that He is fighting for me. I remembered all the times Cozzy would sit with me, sharing stories of when he was in the mob. Cozzy didn't know that every time he sat and talked with me, I would see a father in him. He showed me love. He always bought me coffee and doughnuts for breakfast. At first, I threw them away angrily, but as he continued, I received them with joy and listened to what he had to say.

Sometimes he brought a cake that his wife had baked. Those cakes were delicious! Occasionally, I would tell Cozzy my problems and open up to him as long as he didn't mention anything about Jesus. He gave me advice using Bible verses without letting me know what he was doing. Since I didn't know anything about the Bible or what it said, Cozzy made it sound as if they were his own words; he sounded like a professional counselor.

Without my knowing it, Cozzy was planting the Word of God in my heart. My heart was already becoming softer. I listened to him more and more every day. I told him about the problems I was having with my girlfriend's family. He responded by telling me all the things he went through when he was living that miserable life and all the hell he put his wife through. Every time I talked with him, I felt such a peace. I felt good inside, as if I wanted to stay there listening to all the advice he could give me.

However, as I classified the clutches, the voices continued to aggravate me, growing louder as they told me to kill that day. The whole experience was so demonic that I began to get a migraine headache. I became so frustrated, and my mind was so harassed from hearing those voices that I grabbed the clutches and started to throw them against the wall. I was cursing in a low voice because I didn't want the rest of the workers to hear me as I tried to rid myself of the frustration I was feeling.

As I threw the clutches against the wall, my body began to tremble again. I grabbed the sixth clutch to throw it and couldn't believe what I saw standing before me. About ten feet away was a man in a white robe. His entire robe was as bright as when the sun shines on white snow. His feet were the same color. A cloud covered his face, from his head to his chest.

When I saw him, I backed off and put the clutch on the floor. "What in the world is this?" I asked. As I looked at this man, he lifted up his right hand and pointed at me. He started to speak; his voice came through the cloud. When he spoke, his voice was like thunder; it sounded just like that voice I had heard earlier, which had called me three times by my name.

He said, "My son, it is not you who thinks that way. It is the devil who passes by you."

As soon as he said that, I quickly turned around, thinking, "I know I'm seeing things now. This is not happening to me." I was frightened of what I was seeing. "I know that when I turn around, He is not going to be there." But when I turned around and opened my eyes, He was still standing there. He pointed at me again through the cloud, and he spoke again. My body shook even more.

"My son, I knew you from your mother's womb. I've been with you every day of your life. I am the one fighting this battle for you because I love you, and I am going to use you for my glory." When he said that, he disappeared from in front of me.

I was horribly confused. I couldn't believe what I had just seen. I thought, "No one is going to believe this." I went to the bathroom to change my clothes before I went home. Benny walked into the bathroom, and I told him to tell Cozzy I wasn't feeling well and was going home. Benny saw how very confused and agitated I was. He told me I should tell Cozzy myself, but I asked him to do me the favor. I was leaving because I wasn't feeling well. By the time Cozzy found out, I was already gone.

I drove I-95 South on my way home, but I was still so upset that I drove like a madman. It was eleven in the morning when I finally made it home. I walked in the house, and my mother asked me what was wrong and why I had come home so early. She told me I didn't look at all well.

"I don't know how to tell you this. No one is going to believe me! Mom, a man in a white robe appeared in front of me today at my job. He told me all the evil thoughts I had were not my thinking that way, but they were the devil that passed by me. I was thinking about killing people, Mom, and then blowing myself away; I felt as if I was losing my mind. But when this man appeared, a great peace came upon me, and all those evil thoughts left me. Then he told me that he knew me even when I was in your womb, when I was a little baby. He told me he has a plan for my life, and he wants to use me, Mom. That's what he told me, but I don't know who this man is."

My mother became excited and exclaimed, "Oh, Joey, it's the chief of the Indians! You saw the chief of all the Indians! You are blessed because you have the great Indian with you!"

When I heard *that*, I said to myself, "Man, this woman is really losing her mind. She's crazy. She really believes in that Indian stuff." Then I asked, "Mom, all this stuff about the Indians is real to you, isn't it?"

147

She said to me, "Listen, Joey, if you don't want to believe in it, then *you* are crazy. Don't tell me any more about these things that you are seeing."

Because I arrived home early that day, I called Carmen and told her I needed to talk to her. I told her about the man who appeared to me and about all of the things he said to me. "Carmen, this might sound crazy to you, but I know what I am seeing! And I also know people are going to think I am making this up; they're going to think I am losing my mind, but I'm not. I know I am not crazy."

"I've been in mental hospitals before, but I wasn't crazy then. I have always known exactly what I was doing; the only thing I didn't know was why I did it. I still don't know that. But I do know what I am seeing is true. I keep seeing the dark shadows passing by me, tormenting me, and then I see a man in a white robe who chases the shadows away. Today, I saw that man standing in front of me. I couldn't see his face; a cloud covered it."

Chapter 18

"If I Don't Get Saved"

After I told Carmen everything that had happened to me, she said, "Joey, I believe in my heart that God really is calling you! Maybe He does have a plan for your life, and you're just being stubborn. You don't want to listen; you don't want to surrender."

"How can I trust in God when I don't even believe in Him? How can you tell me about the devil when I don't believe in him either?"

Carmen didn't back down. "The devil is real! When I was in church, I was taught about him and the evil things he does to people."

"Oh, don't tell me you're getting religious on me too!" I said contemptuously. "I have already gone to church with you twice, and nothing has changed. Everything is still the same."

Then she told me I couldn't give up.

I replied, "I don't care about this! I'm just going to keep on living the way I have been." I changed the subject.

Often Carmen listened more than she spoke. But when she did speak, her words were encouraging as she told me to keep striving to go forward, to change; she said I could change. After talking to her, I went down to the neighborhood. I continued to party, get high, and run wild, even though the battle continued inside me. I didn't tell any of my friends what was happening. Whenever I went to the bar, all my friends were waiting for me to give them something to get them high. Philip and his friends still hung out on the corner, getting drunk and starting trouble. I got into trouble with them.

149

Problems with My Girlfriend

Four or five weeks went by after my experience at work. Everything calmed down somewhat, but I became scared to go to work. It seemed as if every time I went there, I became more confused, frustrated, and angry. Whenever I was in the streets, however, nothing like that happened to me.

Today, as a Christian and a minister of the Word of God, I understand how important it was for those twelve Christians to persevere in prayer. They had the key to heaven. I persecuted them, but they were still faithful to their God and their beliefs. They never gave up praying for me. In fact, Cardo's hired Juan Cruz; I remembered Juan from the streets. He was one of the old heads who used to get high in abandoned houses, and he had become close to me. The other Christians, John Gallashore, Juan Lopez, and Benny Holland, couldn't get that close to me; I wouldn't let them. Only Cozzy was able to get through to me, but even with him, I put up a wall.

When I saw Juan Cruz, I noticed that he looked as if he weren't doing drugs anymore. So I asked him how he was doing, and he told me, "Fine!"

Then I saw a Bible in his hands. I asked him, "Are you turning religious too?"

When he said he was, I said, "Man, there's really got to be a God if you became religious! Is God really helping you?"

"Yes, and Joey, I don't care what you say; I know you don't have any peace. I've been here three days, and I've been watching you." Juan was working behind me, taking the plates off the water pumps. "Joe, you look miserable! You're not happy. The other day I saw you with your girlfriend, and I know her family. She's a decent young girl."

I began to open up to him, sharing the problems I had with Carmen's family.

150

"How in the world do you expect them to like you, Joey? Look at the life you're living. Maybe if you got out of that messed up life you're in, they might like you."

I told him I *had* tried to get out of it, and I had even tried to change so that her family would receive me. They rejected me anyway. I told Juan I knew why they didn't like me. "When I was seventeen years old, we were gang warring in front of their house on Fifth and Clearfield Streets. As the gang came down the street, I was hiding behind the church. When they came close to where I was, I jumped out with a shotgun and started to shoot. Her family saw me."

Juan repeated himself, saying, "How do you expect them to like you, Joey, if they saw you shooting at people, trying to kill them?"

"That was then! I'm twenty-two now, and I'm not like that any more. I don't have to kill anyone. If I wanted, I could send people to kill for me."

Juan shook his head. "Joe, you need Jesus! He was the only one who ever gave me hope and peace in my life." Then he began to tell me how he became a Christian, how long he had been free from drugs, and what God was doing for him now. He kept using the phrase "blessed me." He told me how God blessed him. I didn't understand what he meant by that.

Juan didn't have a car; so every day I took him home after work. Every now and then, he too would throw a seed of the Word of God into my heart. Many times I would curse him and tell him I didn't want to hear about Jesus. "If you want me to give you a ride, that's fine, but don't say anything about God! I don't want to hear it."

One day as I went to Carmen's house, I realized that things between us were getting worse. The few times I went to visit her at home, her mother rejected me. As soon as she'd see me park the car, she would go inside the house, angry and upset. Carmen's father was nicer to me. When I spoke to him, he'd answer me and talk with me for awhile.

However, I didn't blame Carmen's mother for the way she treated me, even though it hurt me. Carmen explained that her mother once confided in her that all I wanted to do was get over on Carmen. This was partly true, but I was trying to change. I was really trying. Carmen's mother really loved her and didn't want her to suffer with a man like me. Any mother who would have accepted a man like me for her daughter would have been a fool. And Carmen's mother was no fool.

I asked Carmen, "Do you know me?"

She said, "Yes."

"Do you love me?" "Yes."

I revealed to her that I loved her too, but the stronger my love grew for her, the worse a person I became and the less peace I had. "I don't think I could ever be a good man for you or be faithful to you. Carmen, I don't think I can ever change. You should take your mother's advice and forget about me. I know this is not easy, but I'm doing this for your own good."

Carmen looked at me with tears in her eyes and asked, "What do you mean? That's not what I want. I don't care what my parents say."

"Listen to me, Carmen. I've told you I don't think I can be faithful to you. Why would you want to be with a man who is going to make you suffer? I know I will do just that. You think you are suffering now. I know for a fact that if we get married or run away together, you are going to suffer far more. You'll go through hell because I am going through hell myself. If there is a God, then maybe someday I will change, but right now, I don't think I'm ready. I hope you will remember me for the good times we have had and not for how badly I've treated you or for the kind of person I've been. As of today, I'm going away, and I'm not coming back."

I said this, but it wasn't from my heart. I was crying inside. I hurt because she had put so much hope and faith in

152

me, telling me I could do something better with my life. "When you see me, Carmen, try to act as if you never knew me. Forget about me." I told her I didn't have anyone else in my life. She was the only one. I was doing this for her benefit and for her parents. I walked away from her. Whenever I had been around her, I had felt so dirty and miserable. I didn't want to put her through the same misery.

When I left that day, I found myself in Huntingdon Park on Fourth and Lehigh Streets. Wandy had been with me while I was talking to Carmen but didn't hear anything I said. As we drove away, she asked me what was wrong. I laughed because I thought she was too young to understand these things. However, I told her anyway and said that, as of today, Carmen and I were no longer boyfriend and girlfriend. I said I was going to stay away from Carmen for a few weeks so that we both could think things over and decide what we were going to do.

I just sat there for a while, and then I gave Wandy some money so that she could get a soda from Church's Fried Chicken. When she returned, she asked me why I broke up with Carmen. I said I was no good for her. If I were ever to marry her, I would put her through hell. I didn't know if I even wanted to get married. I had no peace and was tormented at night. I wasn't happy with myself; in fact, I hated myself. How could I love her the way she deserved to be loved if I didn't even love myself?

Wandy answered me, "Joey, you didn't give it a chance. I know she really likes you because she's always talking about you!"

I told Wandy maybe someday Carmen and I would get back together, but right now we needed time to think this over.

Two weeks passed, and I wanted to call Carmen. So I did. I wanted to find out how she was doing. All she did was listen to what I had to say; she was an excellent listener. I began to tell her I was messing around with other girls, but it was a lie. I wanted to kill the love she had in her heart by telling her things like this. The more I told her these lies, the more confused I became.

After three weeks passed, I felt terribly sad inside. I cried and yet was angry at the same time. I began to lose the hope I'd had to change.

"If You Go to the Revival"

One day at work, I found I had tears in my eyes. I was sorting aluminum water pumps and wondering if God could really change me. Was there a God in heaven who could give me peace? Was it really God who had talked to me? Then I thought to myself, "No one can change me, not even Carmen."

Just then, Juan Cruz came running down the aisle, calling my name. When I looked up at him, he too looked as if a cloud covered him. As he reached me, he said, "Joey! God is calling you. You're going to become a good Christian. God is going to use you to bring thousands of souls to his feet."

I grabbed Juan and threw him against the wall, asking, "How do you know what I'm thinking? No one can know that!" Still, I was affected by what he had said.

"Joe, I don't know, but God spoke to me in my heart to tell you that." He walked away.

I began to think once more about Carmen. "Maybe she is the girl for me, or maybe she isn't. Perhaps God just put her there to help me, and there is someone else in my future someday."

I heard Juan again, coming down the aisle, calling my name once more. When he was about seven feet from me, he said, "Joey, the day you surrender your life to the Lord, God holds a woman for you. God already has a wife for you, and He has that woman in His hands. God told me to tell you He holds your future in His hands."

Once again, I grabbed him and threw him against the wall. "How do you know what I'm thinking again? Right now, I was just thinking about my girlfriend, wondering if she was the woman for me or not. And now you come to me, telling me that."

Again Juan told me he didn't know, and he left. Twice more that day, he told me exactly what I was thinking. I became even more confused. During lunch Cozzy shared more with me about God and how He had saved him, called him, delivered him, and used him to talk to other people. Cozzy told me I could be doing the same thing if I were to surrender my life to God. At this stage, I was listening to him more because I was at the end of my rope; there was no other hope for me.

After lunch as I was working, Juan called me again. "Joey, if you go to this revival, you're going to receive Jesus Christ as your Lord and Savior. God is going to set you free!"

I became so angry when I heard the word "free" that I said to him, "I *am* free. What in the world are you talking about?"

"No, Joey," he said, "you're not free. You're bound up by evil. You're bound up by sin. You are bound up by the pleasures of this world, and Jesus Christ wants to set you free. If you go to this revival, you will receive God."

I grabbed him and said, "If I go to this revival and don't receive God, I'm going to kill you and all the other Christians in this company. I'm fed up with this Jesus stuff!"

"No, Joey, you're not going to kill anyone because you are going to receive Jesus!"

I looked at the flyer he had given me. It was about the daughter of Yiye Avila, a well-known evangelist from Puerto Rico. She was promoting his crusades in Philadelphia, and the local churches were having her conduct several revivals herself. I didn't know what this was about; I saw the picture of her holding a microphone with her arm around a girl.

I asked Juan if he was sending me to a discotheque. "I have a whole lot of problems right now; I don't need to go to a party!"

Juan said, "No, Joey! That's Yiye Avila's daughter, and she is going to be preaching tonight. She has fasted forty days and forty nights, and God is using her in healing and deliverance. If you go to that revival, you're going to receive the Lord!"

I became angry with him and cursed him, telling him to get away from me. "Just remember what I told you," I warned. "If I go there and don't receive God, I'm going to kill you and the rest of the Christians here."

After Juan told me about the revival, I said to myself, "Well, I have tried everything, and nothing has worked out for me. Let me try God."

After I got home, I took a shower and changed my clothes. I asked my sister Wandy if she wanted to go with me to the revival. She agreed, and we walked there. When I arrived, I didn't understand anything the woman was saying. All I knew was that it was pouring like crazy that day! It rained so hard that we were soaked even though we had our umbrellas. It looked as if lightening were striking right in front of me, trying to keep me from being there. I stayed for about fifteen minutes, and Wandy got lost among the crowd. After awhile, I walked out, saying that God wasn't real. That was June 6, 1979. I was so frustrated that I began to think seriously about killing all the Christians at my job.

As I left, Wandy called to me, and I saw Carmen standing there with her mother. Her mother motioned toward her as if to say, "He really needs to be here." But I left.

When I got to work the next day, I told Juan to never invite me to another revival. "If you do, I'll kill you for real."

"Joe," he said, "You can't give up!"

I had a great deal of respect for Juan Cruz because he was from our neighborhood. He said, "Joe, go again today!"

"I will, Juan, but remember that if I don't receive God, you and the rest of the Christians here will be dead meat!"

That day, June 7, 1979, on my way home from work, I thought, "If I don't get saved today, this will be the day I kill those seventeen people." I had already planned how I was going to approach them and kill them. I would lure some of them out of their houses, asking them to meet me somewhere, and then I would blow them away. I'd go to Carmen's at five o'clock and kill her and her parents. Before midnight, I would go to my neighborhood, collect the money my drug dealers owed me, take it home, and leave a note stating to whom the money was to go. Then I'd go to South Philadelphia and get the contract to kill the four people. I'd get the forty thousand dollars and give it to my brothers and sisters.

After that, I'd go to the Twenty-fifth District Police Station with two automatic weapons. I would start shooting the police and the detectives who had beaten me and broken my nose. I knew they would begin shooting back. That was how I would die. Tomorrow morning I would be in the papers. Everyone would read about me if God didn't save me that night. The papers would say, "Young man, ex-gang leader and drug dealer, murders seventeen people and dies in a shoot-out with the police." Who knows? Perhaps they would make a movie about my life.

When I arrived home from work, I walked through the door to see my mother sitting in the kitchen with my sisters Vivian and Wandy and my brother Willie. I looked at my mother and said, "You know, Mom, I'm going to get saved today."

She laughed and said jokingly, "You really *need* to get saved! You're losing your mind anyway!"

As I went upstairs, I heard my mother say, "Joey is losing his mind. He's talking about some voice that called him three times by his name. He's saying a man in a white

157

robe appeared before him. I don't know what kind of drugs he's taking. I keep telling him to see the psychiatrist, but he doesn't want to go. Now he's talking about killing seventeen people, including himself. That boy is crazy! I know he'll do it, but what can I do? I'm losing my mind too just thinking about it. I don't even have peace at night when I go to sleep, thinking about what he might do."

I heard her say all that. I took a shower and got dressed. "Well, if I don't get saved today, then this is it." My rifle and my gun were ready.

Chapter 19

No Longer the Devil's Child

I had some drugs in my pocket I was planning to sell. I was dressed well that day; I wore a pair of tailor-made jeans, a pair of $150 shoes, and a designer shirt. But I felt dirty and filthy inside. As I was ready to walk out of the bedroom, I stopped and went to the window. Opening it up, I said, "God, I'm going to this revival, and if you are real, I want you to say this. I don't care how you say it. 'Tonight there is a young man with a good blessing from the Lord, and that young man's name is José.' If you say this, God, no rain, no snow, no fire, no devil, no demon, no one is going to stop me. I'll receive you tonight."

As I was saying this, I heard my mother downstairs say to my sister, "I told you that boy is crazy. Now he's upstairs calling on God."

When I came downstairs, I told her once more that I was going to get saved. She told me, "What you need is to see a psychiatrist! Why are you going to that revival? Come here."

As I looked at her, I noticed that a dark cloud covered her face. I rejected what she was saying and started walking to the revival. It was still drizzling, and I thought about what Juan told me earlier. "Joey, on your way to the revival, you're going to find girls and guys who will offer you drugs. Some will try to lure you into their houses and try to seduce you. But remember this: All of it is the devil trying to stop you from receiving God."

I lived between American and Third Streets on Westmoreland. I got to Third and Allegheny, where there was a little fish shop. As I passed by the shop, going under the railroad tracks, three young girls were getting high there. As soon as they saw me, they called me over. I couldn't understand why they did that; these girls were somewhat conservative, and they hated me and were scared of me. They asked me if I wanted to get high with them. Walking over, I just stared at them, thinking, "These girls never talk to me. They hate me, but now they're asking me to get high with them!"

They lit two sticks of marijuana and began to puff on them; I couldn't believe what they were doing. Then I said to them, "You know something? You belong to the devil! That's right! Juan told me this was going to happen."

When I said that, they looked at me as if I were crazy, turned around, and started to run. I heard one of them say, "What did he say? Man, he's really crazy! He's losing his mind! He said something about the devil."

In the meantime, I crossed Allegheny from the north to the south side, drawing close to Fifth Street. There used to be a gas station on the corner, and as I took a shortcut through it, I heard a car pull up, burning rubber. Thinking it was someone who was going to shoot me, I went to pull out my gun, only to realize I didn't have it with me. When I looked, I saw two guys, Bee and Pete, get out of the car. They used to call me Killer.

They called me over to their car, and as I walked up, I noticed there were three girls sitting in the back of the car. One of them kept smiling at me, and I could hear them whispering about me. Bee continued to talk to me, speaking rapidly, "Come on, Joe! We've got three girls in the car. There are only two of us, and we need another guy. We're going to Atlantic City and then to a hotel, and you know we're going to have some fun with these girls! All you need is something to get high with!"

I didn't have much money on me. I told them that, and they said they would take care of everything. However, as they talked to me, all I could hear was Juan's voice telling me, "It's the devil. It's the devil." I tried to reject that voice and was ready to step into the car when I heard that voice clearly: "It's the devil!"

160

I pulled my foot back out of the car and thought, "Wait a minute! These guys never invite me to go anywhere with them. The only time they want me around is when they get into trouble with someone and want me to take care of business for them. And now, all of a sudden, they're inviting me to go with them all expenses paid?"

I said to them, "You know what? You belong to the devil. Get out of my face." They all looked at each other, trying to figure out what happened. They shut the car door and took off.

I kept walking down Fifth Street to the revival. As I got closer to Clearfield, I saw Carmen's oldest brother sitting on their house steps. We didn't like each other at all. The only people in Carmen's family who got along with me were her little brother and her sister Susie.

I turned right on Clearfield, going toward Sixth Street to the schoolyard, where they were having the revival. I had an earring in my left ear and a few sticks of marijuana stuck in my hair. I had just shaved off my beard, leaving a goatee. I had my coat over my left arm and my umbrella on the right. I strutted all the way to the front. People looked at me, wondering what I was doing there. Walking toward the front, I felt very uneasy and dirty. As the woman evangelist began to preach, I understood some of the things she was saying, especially when she talked about murderers, drug addicts, and dealers. I couldn't understand everything, but I got the general idea of her message. As she spoke, I began to feel even more uncomfortable, dirty, and out of place.

Standing there with my arms crossed, I said, "Okay, God! I'm here. Now, where are You?"

Suddenly, an older woman came up to me and asked me how I was doing. She was joyful, and she gave me a hug and a kiss on the cheek.

I thought, "This woman is crazy! She doesn't even know who I am!" Then another woman came up and asked me how I was doing. She also hugged me. I thought they were really crazy! I was sure they didn't know me but were confusing me with someone else. After that, the woman who was preaching said something, and the whole crowd began cheering. It was as if she had pressed a button, and in unison all the people began to shout and raise their hands to the sky. I thought that perhaps Jesus had come! I was expecting to see a man in a white robe come down from the sky in a chariot and park it on the platform!

Not knowing what had happened, I saw people look toward the sky, and I figured they had seen Him coming down. One woman was saying, "Thank you, Jesus! Thank you, Jesus!" and throwing kisses into the air; that really flipped me out.

I thought, "Man, if my friends see me with these Christians, they're going to say I'm crazy too. Let me out of here!" I figured I could hide by a wall near me; I stood there for a while, looking around to see if any of my friends were in the crowd. So many people were there that night; I saw one person I thought looked like Juan Cruz. As I looked closer, I realized it actually was Juan. He waved at me. Maybe he was there to make sure I got saved that night. After all, I had told him if I didn't get saved I was going to kill him and the rest of the Christians at work!

Standing closer to the wall, I could hear noise, as if people were mumbling. Looking to my right, I saw fifteen to twenty elderly people praying, kneeling on the concrete. They were praying and interceding for the woman preaching that night, Naomi Avila. As I listened to these people praying, I felt even dirtier and more uncomfortable. I heard voices telling me to leave. "Joe, get out of here. God isn't real. Go now, Joey, go now! Leave! Go kill those seventeen people!" These voices started to torment me, taking away the little peace I had. Suddenly, I screamed, "God ain't real!"

162

His Name Is José!

I cursed, turned around, and started to walk away from the revival, pushing people out of my way. I almost reached the end of the schoolyard when Naomi Avila stopped her message. Silence fell upon everyone there. You literally could have heard a pin drop.

"Hey you, young man! Hold it!"

I stopped instantly when she yelled that! I thought without speaking, "Is she talking to me?"

"Yeah, you!" When Naomi Avila said that, I felt cold chills from my head to my toes. Was I scared! Then she continued, "Tonight, there is a young man here with a good blessing from the Lord, *and that young man's name is Jose*" When she said that, I turned around, facing the crowd. The crowd turned around and was facing me! Again she called out, "Young man, you said if God called you this way, no rain, no snow, no fire, no devil, no demon, nothing was going to stop you."

"Hold up!" I said to myself. "It's really God! That woman doesn't know me." I tried to run to the front, but I couldn't. I tried again, and still I could not. A battle began inside me. As it raged, I reasoned that if I got saved I couldn't run around with women as I had done. I couldn't sell drugs or collect drug money. "If I get saved tonight, no one is going to respect me. People know I won't be able to shoot anyone or be violent toward someone who tries to hurt me."

Another thought entered my mind: "But with all this, I'm not happy anyway!" I tried to take a step to go up front, but I couldn't. I said within myself, "God help me! I know it's You!"

Then I heard a voice say, "Now!" Entering my ear like a tiny wind, the voice surged through my body like an echo. It kept repeating, "Now, now, *now*, NOW!" As it echoed, I felt a burden lift from me. I started to run toward

163

the front.

No one was making an altar call, but I went forward anyway, running and crying out, "Here I come, God! Here I come, God!" I still had the umbrella in my right hand and the coat in my left as I ran to the altar. People moved out of my way! As Naomi Avila saw me running toward her with the umbrella, she began to back off, thinking I was coming to hurt her. I took the umbrella and the coat, threw them on the ground, and called out, "God! I'm here! I've shed blood. I've done a lot of bad things. Lord, I'll do whatever you want; just make me happy!"

My body started to tremble; tears were running down my face, and I was crying like a baby. I said, "God, if You want, I'll preach for You. I'll do whatever you want, just make me happy. Set me free tonight, Lord. Be the Lord and Savior of my life."

When I said that, a soothing feeling went through my body. It felt as if electricity were running through my arms. It continued to move through my body and around my face. Often I had felt as if another person were inside me, but once the electricity hit my toes, my body jerked and something dark came out of me. I felt brand new inside — clean as never before! When I arrived at the revival, I had felt so dirty, but all that changed; I felt so clean. Suddenly, I started to feel as if my body were burning. It was like a fire burning my flesh, but it wasn't painful; it was a comforting feeling. I was being baptized in the Holy Spirit's fire and power.

Opening my eyes, I found myself standing in front of three thousand people. I began to pinch my arms and shake my head. I could see people next to me, but they sounded as if they were far away. I sensed I was in the glory and presence of God. I believe the sensation of electricity, which ran down my body, was the blood of Jesus, cleansing me from all my sins. It began to break the generational curse over me, which had been handed down from my ancestors. My father's history was one of stabbing and shooting people, but those curses were being broken over my life. I began to shout and sob and jump around, crying, "I'm free! I'm free! *I'm free!*"

People looked at me, and I could hear them saying, "What's wrong with that young man? What happened to him?" A girl standing at the front exclaimed, "Look! He's not shaking any more." I cried and thanked God in front of all those people, not feeling embarrassed or ashamed before them.

I continued to shout, "Thank you, Jesus! Thank you, Jesus!" Then, I closed my eyes and knelt on the ground, thanking Him from within. That soothing, comforting spirit enveloped me. When I opened my eyes again and looked around, almost a hundred people stood at the altar with me, and no one had to do an altar call! Naomi Avila had us repeat the sinner's prayer. Loudly, I repeated it after her, filled with excitement. I walked over to the counselors and gave them my name and address.

Leaving the revival, people hugged me; it seemed no one was scared of me. Many of them knew who I was. People from churches in my own neighborhood hugged me too; they were happy for me.

"Your Face Is Glowing!"

Walking home, I found myself singing a song the whole way. When I walked into my house, I beamed at my mother and said, "Mom! Guess what? I received Jesus tonight! Mom, I feel really good." Tears filled my eyes as I continued, "I feel good because He forgave me, Mom. He forgave me!"

My mother looked at me and said, "Joey, your whole face is shining. You're glowing!"

I told Mom how He called me by my name. I went to my room, took a shower, and went to sleep. It was the first time in my life I slept so well. In fact, I slept so well that I woke up late! I called Cozzy and told him that I was running late and that I had something good to tell him.

Finally arriving at work, I walked through the door, and Cozzy stared at me. "Cozzy, guess what?"

"Joe, what happened? Your whole face is glowing. Look at you; you look brand new."

I explained what had happened. "Cozzy, last night I received Jesus! Jesus called me by my name in a revival. I told Him if He called me by name, I would receive Him."

Tears ran down Cozzy's face; he grabbed me and kissed me on my right and left cheeks — his Italian custom. I wasn't used to that! "Joe, I told you that if you would give Him a chance He would give you peace." I was so excited and overwhelmed that Cozzy called Benny, John, Juan Lopez, and the rest of the Christian guys. "Joe received the Lord! He received the Lord!"

All the guys who weren't Christians came up to the front to find out what had happened. Even they could see I looked different. They asked, "What happened? You look different today!"

Juan Cruz joined us, saying, "You know, I was there! The Lord called him by his name. The woman who was preaching said, 'Tonight, there is a young man with a good blessing from the Lord, and that young man's name is José.' I had a feeling it was him!"

I related to Juan how I bargained with God in my room: If He called me that way, I would receive Him. Everyone was happy, and I was excited and full of joy. I was saved on Tuesday night, June 7, 1979, and the very next day I was already telling people about Jesus Christ.

I told Bob I didn't want any more drugs. I flushed a large quantity I still had down the toilet. I didn't even go down into the neighborhood to collect my drug money; I let it all go to waste. I stayed away from the guys in my neighborhood for a while. I began to witness to the guys on my job. Every time I went home, I would pray and pray. I didn't have a local church, so one of the guys at work, Sam Toland, another Christian guy I used to hate and tried to kill, offered for me to go with him until I found one where I could grow in the Lord.

Chapter 20

Transformation

I decided to accompany Sam to his church on Sunday morning. Saturday night I knelt down in prayer. "I don't know what to do, Lord. I just accepted You. I don't know where to go. Thank You that John Gallashore is helping me know more about You." John had taken it upon himself to teach me the Word of God. "Lord, I need your help. I need a church. And I also need a Bible because I don't even have one."

Sunday morning I went to Sam Toland's church on Twenty-second and Berks, right on the corner: Mt. Pisgah Church. That morning Sam didn't make it to church because he had to go out of town. Upon sitting down, an elderly woman sat next to me, asking me who I was. I said I worked with Sam and had accepted Jesus on Tuesday. Sam had told me to come to his church until I could find a local church of my own to attend.

The woman got one of the deacons in the church; he asked me if I understood the decision I had made. I told him yes; I made a decision to serve God from now on. He then asked me if I knew Jesus Christ died on the cross for my sins. And I told him yes; He had cleansed me with His blood. The deacon asked me if I had a Bible, and I told him I did not. He was trying to find out if I had made a true confession of faith to serve Jesus from now on. He gave me a Bible. Excitedly I exclaimed, "I asked God for a Bible last night, and look! He gave me one!"

The deacon replied, "Son, you are going to learn many things about God you never knew before. You are going to ask God for more things, and He is going to give them to you to show you that He is God. I'd like to take you in front of the congregation and introduce you to everyone." Leading me to the front of the church, he introduced me as a friend of Sam Toland.

"Sam has been sharing the Gospel with me, and I accepted the Lord Tuesday night," I explained. "Now I'm a new brother in Christ!"

Everyone at the church began praising God. Several stood up, came over, and hugged me. That was something I wasn't used to; not too many people had ever hugged me. I began to feel wanted and loved by these people. I had caught the bus to go to church, but I walked all the way back home, about forty city blocks. I left the church so happy that I sang a song; people looked at me as I walked along trying to figure me out.

The day I was saved I wrote a song to the Lord. As I walked down the street, I was singing that song with no fear of death.

A Quick Work

When I reached Glenwood and Germantown Streets, some guys standing there saw me with my Bible. They called me over. As I walked closer, one of them said, "Yo! What's that you've got in your hands?" He was talking like a gangster, and he had a quart of beer in his hand. I still had that rough talk and look about me.

I said to him sarcastically, "What do you think it is?"

"Let me see it," he said. "Do you know anything about it?"

"No," I told him, "I just accepted the Lord on Tuesday." I took the Bible and handed it to him.

He told me, "You start reading from Genesis all the way to Revelation."

"Oh, okay," I replied.

When I asked him to give it back to me, he said, "No! I'm not going to give it back to you. I don't like Puerto Ricans."

As soon as he said that, I was ready to hit him; however, I said, "I don't care who you like or not. Give me back my Bible." He pulled it away from me again. "I'm going to tell you something," I said. "At one time, I didn't like blacks, whites, or Puerto Ricans either. Before I became a Christian, I shot people. I was a drug dealer and a gang leader. I've been in jail for a lot of things; if you don't give me my Bible, I'm going to kill you right now." I snatched it from his hands.

He was scared, and he backed off. "You did all that?" he asked.

"Yes, and you'd better thank God I'm saved. Otherwise, I would have blown you away right here!"

"Wow!" he replied. "You don't look like that kind of guy!" That's how fast the Lord was working in my life; I'd only been a Christian five days, and people could already see a change in my life. Then he said, "You know, someday I might see you in heaven. If God can change you, He can change anyone."

I walked away, singing again. I arrived home happy and excited.

The day of the revival, God set me free from drugs and everything else, except cigarettes. I began to cut back on them, and three weeks later the Lord delivered me from them also. I visited Sam Toland's church again; I came under so much conviction during the preaching that I threw the cigarettes in the trash when I got home. From that day, I never smoked again.

My car needed some work. My cousin Felipe and his brother-in-law, Carmelo, were doing body and fender work on my car. When I went to see how much they had left to do on it, Carmelo told me they needed a part. I went with them to Camden, New Jersey, to look for the part. Carmelo and his wife, Olga, were Christians who attended a Baptist Church on Seventh Street and Erie Avenue.

While returning from Camden, driving north on Fifth Street, we saw a church — Temple Sinai Assembly of God. My cousin Felipe said, "Joey, that church would be a good one for you to attend." The night before I had asked the Lord to show me a church I could attend. I needed a home church.

I looked at Carmelo and thought, "Wait a minute! These guys are Christians. They go to a Baptist Church, and since I got saved, they haven't even invited me to their church. Maybe God is answering my prayer, and He wants me to go to that church instead." That night when I got home, I began to pray. I often prayed so loud that the neighbors would hear me. Every day I prayed and cried. I couldn't understand how God could forgive me after I had committed so many crimes and had hurt so many people. As I was praying, I told the Lord I was going to that church on Fifth and Somerset Streets. If He wanted me there, then I would feel comfortable and at home as soon as I walked through the doors.

Sunday morning I went to that church, which used to be an old movie theater. There were about four hundred members. As I sat in the back of the church, a man walked over to me and asked if I was a visitor.

"Yes," I said, "and I'm looking for a home church."

He asked me if I was a Christian, and I told him I had accepted the Lord about four weeks earlier but had not yet found a church. He brought another man, named Amador Rolon, over to meet me. I asked him if he owned the Photo Studio on Fifth Street. He replied that it belonged to his brother Luis and asked me if I was from Fifth and Indiana Streets. When I told him I was, he said, "That's a bad neighborhood."

I replied, "Yes, I know! I was a gang leader and a drug dealer in that neighborhood. But four weeks ago, I accepted Jesus Christ as my Lord and Savior."

"Praise God," Amador told me. "When you said that, I felt goose bumps."

He took me to his youth class. There were about fifty young people in the class; nine were guys, and the rest were girls — very pretty, young Christian girls. Even though they were pretty, they didn't attract my attention. I was still in love with Carmen. I was thinking about seeking the Lord by myself first, and if it were God's will, Carmen would be there with me, serving the Lord too.

When the offering was taken up, everyone was putting in fifty cents or a dollar. I had about fifteen hundred dollars on me from someone who had owed me money and had paid up even though I wasn't collecting anymore. I took fifty dollars and placed it in the offering. I was wearing two gold chains around my neck, a gold watch, and a ring with seventeen diamonds, tailor-made pants, and a very nice shirt. People looking at me probably thought I was rich.

When the class was finished, Amador's sister Judy came up to me and began to talk to me. She asked me several questions about how I got saved. Then Judy's brother and some other people asked me questions as well. Some said they remembered when I got saved because they were at the revival as well. One thing I did know; I was becoming very comfortable with them. I saw many young people there, and I felt it would be a blessing for me to be in this church; perhaps I could help some of these people not to go astray and live the life I lived in the past.

I went home happy from church. When I arrived at home, I prayed and thanked the Lord for that church and asked Him to help me help the young people there. "Help me be a blessing to them, Lord."

Every day that I went to work I arrived early to pray. Cozzy and the rest of the Christians helped me learn more about God. During the lunch break, I would go into an empty office, kneel, and pray. Cozzy and the others began to teach me that I needed to fast so that the rest of the chains would be broken from my life.

I began to fast almost daily, skipping breakfast and lunch. Then I fasted two or three days out of the week. I had a heart to do God's will. The more I went to Sinai Assembly of God on Fifth and Somerset Streets, the more I liked it. The pastor there called me into his office one day and began to talk to me. I could hardly understand what he was saying, and I couldn't understand much of what he preached because everything was in Spanish. The only thing that really helped me was Sunday school because the class was in English. Every Sunday after the service, I would grab a handful of tracts and give them to people on my way home.

Some members of the church wanted me to go home with them to fellowship, but I would decline the invitation by telling them I needed to win souls. On my way home, I stopped to witness to people. God quickly began to use me; as I told them about Him, they often began to weep. Sometimes I would see my friends shooting dice, and I would break up their games. I wanted everyone to know about my Jesus! When I broke up the dice games, they wouldn't say anything because they thought I was still crazy. Even though I was a Christian, they thought I would backslide someday. Still, they listened to what I had to say. Even guys who had been my enemies, whom I had hurt in the past, would stop when they saw me with a Bible and asked all kinds of questions.

The first three months I was saved, by the grace of God, I had sixty families coming to the church. I was always bringing someone with me. One day the pastor asked me to share my testimony. No one really knew what had happened to me and how I had gotten saved. Many people in the church didn't know what kind of person I had been in my past. I invited Cozzy to hear me share my testimony.

It was a Friday night. Cozzy brought a sergeant of police and another man, a captain in the army, who were his friends and Christian brothers. They wanted to hear my testimony also. I had never spoken in front of people before, and I was scared to get up in front of people. I was used to talking one-on-one or with just a few people but not a whole group.

In preparation, I fasted and prayed for three days. That night I thanked God that I didn't feel as nervous as I thought I would. I already had in mind what I was going to say. I thought it would take about a half-hour. But when I stood in front of those people and saw how many had come to hear me, including John Gallashore and Bob, a co-worker, I became so nervous. I think it took me only five minutes to give my entire testimony!

I was nervous and spoke rapidly without taking a breath. After I finished, Cozzy congratulated me and told me to keep doing a good work. God was going to use me. Many people told me God had a plan for my life, but I didn't understand what they meant when they said this. That night I couldn't sleep. I felt so embarrassed. I tried to remember what I had said, but I couldn't because I had spoken so fast. I prayed that God would show me how to give my testimony and take away the fear I felt in front of people. As I continued to pray, the Lord helped me overcome my fear. He taught me things I needed to know from His Word.

An Old Friend

One night in a Sunday evening service, my friend Edwin Colon, whom we called Lemon, came to church. I used to sit in the fifth row from the front of the church. I was sitting there, waiting for the preaching to begin, when I saw Edwin come in. I gave him a hug and was happy to see him there. Lemon belonged to my gang and committed a crime the same night I was almost killed at the discotheque. Back then, I had walked Lemon home, and everyone in his family was crying. They wanted me to tell him to give himself up. Instead, I told him I would give him some money to get out of the city. However, Lemon decided to give himself up, and he wanted me to be there when he did. Instead, I hid around the corner and watched as they took him away to jail.

A few months later, Lemon made bail, and he got out of prison, waiting to go to court. When he got out of jail, I saw him with a Bible, and I became really angry with him; I even called him a hypocrite. I told him he was just trying to get his sentence reduced by pretending to be a Christian. However, I saw him going to Mt. Sinai Assembly of God Church on Fifth and Somerset. Whenever I saw him coming out of church, I'd try to get away from him. A few times he came to my house to witness to me, but I grabbed him by the hand, walked him off the porch, and told him I didn't want to hear what he had to say. He was supposed to be following me, not Jesus!

Lemon received a fourteen-month sentence and left jail three weeks before I accepted Jesus as my Savior. When I saw him come out of jail, I told him to keep serving God and to continue to go to church, but he didn't. He backslid and never came back to church.

I had been saved for about four months when he came to the service that night. Afterward, I gave him a hug; I could see he was very far away from God. He had been backslidden for almost five months. He sat in the service for only a little while. I could tell he felt very uncomfortable while the preacher was preaching. He could not sit still. Suddenly, Lemon patted me on the shoulder and said words I will never forget, "Joey, I'm leaving. I can't stay here. I don't feel right." I tried to convince him to stay, but he was determined to leave. "Joey, I came to tell you that whatever you do, don't ever go back to the old life. I want to be here with you. I want to serve the Lord, but I just can't come back. The devil has a hold on me, Joe." I could see tears in his eyes as he talked to me. He turned around and walked away. As he did, my heart broke because I knew he wanted to be here, serving the Lord.

175

However, I found his words encouraging. As I grew in the Lord, I began to change. There were many young girls and guys who came to me for advice and counsel. I would talk to these young girls in front of everyone, telling them that whatever they did, "Don't go out there! There's nothing for you there." I shared what I had been like and that the same kinds of guys were still out there. Some of their mothers saw me talking to them, and the mothers would pull their daughters away from me. The mothers didn't want me anywhere near their girls.

At first, I thought it was my imagination, but then I realized it was not. It was really happening. There were some mothers in the church who actually thought I was trying to get over on their daughters. After they heard my testimony, they knew what kind of man I had been, and they had their doubts about me. Even though there were many girls in the church, I wasn't interested in any of them.

There were still so many things I didn't understand about the Lord; I called the pastor to seek his counsel. Then I found out the elderly people in the church had a prayer service, and I decided I needed to get involved with them in prayer. I was almost twenty-three. Every Monday and Wednesday night these elderly people got together to pray from seven to nine o'clock. I began attending their prayer services with them, noticing there weren't any young people there.

However, I also noticed that these older people had what I wanted. They had the knowledge of the Word, and I wanted to learn more about Jesus. I wasn't thinking at all about having a girlfriend.

Chapter 21

Called to His Work

Even though I had broken up with Carmen, I kept praying that if she wasn't God's will for my life, He would take away the feelings I still had for her. I wanted to please God in every area. I was so much in love with Jesus that I couldn't think about a girl at that time. I wanted to win souls for Him! I wanted to let people know about Jesus Christ.

At the prayer services, those elderly Christians would pray for two hours on their knees. After thirty-five minutes, I was finished. What else should I pray for? However, I was praying the Lord would baptize me with the Holy Spirit so that I could speak with new tongues, according to what the Scriptures say. I wanted to experience more of God.

After thirty-five minutes, I wasn't praying anymore. Nevertheless, I stayed there kneeling, pretending I was praying because I felt ashamed that these older people could stay on their knees much longer than I could. I began to pick up some of their prayers and add them to mine; the next thing I knew, I was praying for about an hour. Then it became longer, an hour and a half and then two hours. I became addicted to prayer. I couldn't wait for Monday and Wednesday to come around so that I could go to church to pray with these elderly people.

The young people saw me with them and asked me what I was doing "hanging around with the old folks. They're not into anything. All they do is pray!"

I told them, "That's exactly what I want to do." There were many times after we finished praying that I would ask them questions. I would sit there with about fifteen elderly people and ask them all kinds of questions about God. I shared my problems with them; every day I kept repenting from my sins. I think I felt I was doing something wrong. There were times I would witness to people who didn't want

177

to listen; I would grab them by the collar and push them up against the wall. Then I would tell them they had to listen to me whether they liked it or not. People were still scared of me.

I thought I was doing the right thing. I wanted *everyone* to know — willingly or by force — what Jesus had done for me! I thank God for those older Christians who advised me, telling me this really wasn't the way to witness to people. They told me to continue to seek the Lord and to keep reading the Bible, and God would show me how to win souls for him. I always told people all I wanted to do was win souls for Jesus. I told these elderly people I would read the Bible, but often I couldn't understand it. They told me how to pray and what to pray for. The most important thing they told me was to pray for wisdom, knowledge, and understanding of the Word of God and of His Spirit.

It was spring, and I had been saved for seven months. I wanted to do something with the young people from church; instead, I heard that the adults were doing street meetings. They asked if I wanted to be the preacher one particular day. I didn't know what to say because I didn't know how to preach. I remembered sharing my testimony in church and how I felt that day; I didn't want to go through that again.

After fasting again for three days, I went to the street meeting anyway. I told Cozzy, John Gallashore, and the rest of the Christian guys from my job to keep me in prayer because I was going to preach at a street meeting. To the best of my ability, I was prepared. I prayed, fasted, and was ready to go out there and preach. As the day drew closer, I prayed it would rain and storm because I was scared! I didn't want to be in front of all those people again.

"I Am That Woman"

The meeting was to take place on the corner of Fourth and Indiana Streets. This was the same corner where I used to sell drugs. I used to get drunk in the corner bar. We arrived there, and it was time for me to share. I gave my entire testimony in ten minutes. Again, I don't remember what I said because I was speaking so fast.

When I got home that night, the devil started to attack me. I couldn't sleep. I felt embarrassed. The devil told me I was stupid and dumb. Why did I preach like that? That's not the way you preach! After that street meeting, I couldn't sleep for two whole months. I battled spirits every night. I would be lying in bed and feel the mattress being pushed away from me. I would go downstairs trying to find some relief but instead, I found my mother was being used by the devil. She would curse me and tell me to go to hell with God.

One day my brother Philip walked in the house; I had just finished a fast, and he ripped off his shirt and threw it in my face. I jumped up ready to punch him in the face when I heard my mother say, "Joey, don't do it." Looking at Philip, I could see the devil in him. He was breathing hard and cursing me.

I told him, "I'm not even going to hit you. You know, Jesus loves you."

As soon as I said that, he said, "Shut up!"

"Wow," I thought to myself, "this thing really works!" Then I said it again. "Jesus loves you." He told me to shut up and turned his face away from me. I said it the third time, "Jesus loves you," and he turned and walked out the door.

When he left, I went to my room and lay on my bed, but I couldn't sleep. Suddenly, Philip came back into the house, and I heard him say to my mother, "I don't know why I bother Joey. Ever since he got saved, I feel as if I envy him. Even though I'm embarrassed about the decision he has

179

made, I'm also happy for him. Everyone is saying Joey is crazy. Now he stands on the street corners saying God saved him, and he's going into the discotheques telling people Jesus wants to save them. He even stops the DJ from playing music because he has something to say. He starts talking about Jesus, and no one stops him; they're all scared of him. They think he has lost his mind. He even goes up to people who are ready to fight, and he stops them to tell them about Jesus. I don't know why I bother him. I'm really happy for him." He didn't know I could hear everything he said to my mother.

One Wednesday night when I went to church for the prayer service, I shared with the people there that I couldn't go to sleep after the street meeting. They told me I didn't have to speak so fast. I just needed to take my time. God was going to help me. He was going to use me because He knew the zeal in my life. He had a plan for my life!

In the prayer group was a woman named Sister Gonzalez. She was about sixty-five years old and very pretty. There was something about her that used to bother me; she was always staring at me. In every prayer service the people prayed for me and anointed me with oil. They prayed I would receive the gift of tongues. I loved that group of elderly people because I was learning so much from them; I was growing in the Lord.

One particular night Sister Gonzalez walked over to me and asked, "Joey, can I ask you a question? Did you once have an afro, a beard, and a big earring?"

"Yes, I did. Why do you ask?"

"Joey, I want to ask you another question. Did you used to hang out on the corner of Fourth and Indiana Streets?

"Yes," I told her, "I used to be a gang leader and a drug dealer in that neighborhood."

Then she said, "Joey, about a year ago there was a woman who went to witness to a young man there."

180

"Yes," I replied, "I remember that. A woman came to me to tell me God was calling me. God told her to go to that corner because there was a young man He wanted to save, and that man was me. That day I was ready to kill one of my drug dealers, and she gave me some tracts. I was so angry at her because she had interrupted me from killing this guy that I took the tracts and threw them in her face."

"Joey," she said, "I am that woman." When she said that, we both began to cry. "Joey, ever since that day, even though I didn't know the young man's name, I prayed to God, saying, 'Lord, whoever that young man is, save him, God. Save him, God.'" The tears ran down her face. "Ever since you have been coming to our church, I kept looking at you because you looked so much like him. I wasn't sure if you were the same man or not. Joey, this is a joy! God answers prayers in a miraculous way. I didn't stop praying that God would save you, and now you are here."

I hugged Sister Gonzalez. "Sister, thank you, thank you so much for praying for me. Thank you for not giving up on me."

Everyone came up to us and heard what we were talking about. They asked me to share my testimony again with the whole congregation because they wanted to hear how I got saved. That Sunday night I shared my testimony. That time I took my time and shared for about twenty minutes. I told them how the Lord called me by my name and how He appeared in front of me. I also told them how God had used Sister Gonzalez to tell me He was calling me.

After I finished my testimony, they had an altar call. About twenty-five people got saved. Then Pepe Nieves, a real prayer warrior, came to me and said, "Joey, God is going to use you mightily, and you don't even know it." He continued, "You already have the gifts; they just have to come to a fullness. God is going to use you to win thousands of souls for him. As you were sharing your testimony, the Lord showed me that."

181

The following month the pastor came to me and asked me into his office. He told me that at the evening service they were going to anoint me as the youth evangelist of the church. "Joey, God has used you tremendously since you've been here. The church has grown because you have brought so many people here. You have brought people here whom I don't think any of us would have reached. God is using you to bring people in; we want to anoint you as an evangelist in this church."

That night Pastor brought me before the entire congregation and said, "This young man has been here for eight months, and God has used him tremendously. I want to anoint him as the youth evangelist of this church so that he can work with the young people, taking them out into the streets to witness to others."

Two or three people figured I wasn't ready or prepared enough to be anointed as the youth evangelist. You will always find these kinds of people in the church. They don't do anything but complain. However, Pastor and the elders anointed me anyway.

The same night they anointed me, I asked the church if they wanted to go out with me to do a street meeting. I also asked Pastor if I could use the sound equipment for the meeting. There were five young men who were saved out of the gangs as well. One of them was Joshua; another was Angel, the brother of one of my ex-girlfriends named Maria. I took these five young men and some of the other young people from the church with me. Every Monday, Wednesday, and Saturday we were out in the streets winning souls.

Some of the adults also joined us, including Catalina Rolon, who became my spiritual mother, and her walky, Sister Isabel; they were always together. After we prayed on Mondays, Wednesdays, and Saturdays, we would go to the streets to do a street meeting. On Sundays, Tuesdays, and Thursdays we had church services. I kept myself busy with the things of God. I knew this would help me stay away from the world and close to God. We continued to do street meetings, and the more we did, the more churches became involved with us. Different churches asked me to come to their church to share what God had done for me. I always asked my pastor if it was all right with him; he never hindered me from going to another church to share my testimony.

My pastor also told me our church had a Bible institute and encouraged me to go to it. I began to attend the institute, but because everything was in Spanish, I was really confused. I had been saved about eight months when I enrolled. After being in the Bible institute for two months, I felt I wasn't learning anything because of the language barrier. I paid the tuition, but the teachers realized I wasn't grasping the lessons. They continued to encourage me to come. Even though I probably wasn't learning much about the Word, I was learning the language! I kept on going.

When I had been saved for eight months, I held a big youth rally. I shared some of my testimony and brought other speakers to preach the Word of God, people such as Nino Gonzalez and Edwin Martinez. The entire church was being stirred up, and the young people and the adults were becoming involved.

God's Plans for Me

A brother named Angel Robles from our church finished Bible college. Even though he was pastoring a church in Lansdale, Pennsylvania, he had a burden to start a men's drug rehabilitation center. He felt led by the Lord to stop pastoring and begin the drug program because there was such a need in Philadelphia. He came to me one day and told me he needed to talk with me. He didn't know that I had just been on a three day fast, during which I saw him in a vision coming to my house to speak with me.

Exactly as I saw him in the vision, he knocked on the door, and I opened it. Shocked to see him there, I said, "I have been fasting, and I saw you coming to my house. I'm supposed to help you do something. I don't know what it is, but here I am."

Chapter 22

His Perfect Will

Angel Robles was excited when he heard that and said, "I've come here to tell you I'm going to start a men's rehabilitation program. Can you give me a hand with it? I'm going to need some assistance in starting it, and I believe you can be a great help to me in the program."

I replied that I would think about it. My mother was all for it right away because she felt it would be good for me. It was time to move out of my mother's house. I was having so many problems there; spiritually, it wasn't helping me any. An uncle of mine rented me an apartment on Thirteenth and Westmoreland Streets. A brother in my church named Ruben moved in with me, and we shared the rent. Ruben happened to be Angel Robles' brother-in-law.

Around that time, I asked Cozzy to let me go if a lay off ever came. He didn't want to, but I explained to him that I wanted to help this brother in the church start a men's rehabilitation center. Cozzy replied, "Joey, it is because the Lord is telling me to let you go that I'm doing it. You're not the next in line to be laid off, but you have to do what the Lord is telling you." He laid me off, and I collected unemployment.

Now I was free to work with Angel Robles in the program. We had a service in our church, and about a thousand people came to it. Robles preached, and I gave a hundred dollars in the offering. The rest of the people followed in the giving. We collected an offering of nearly three thousand dollars to buy the house we needed for the program.

About a month later, Angel Robles asked me if I could move in with the guys because he needed a live-in staff. Ruben had moved out of the apartment; I was living there by myself. At the same time, my brother Edwin was having problems with his wife. They were losing the apartment in which they lived; I asked them to stay in my apartment and continue to pay the rent. Leaving everything in it, I went to live in the men's center with the five guys who were already there. We picked these guys up from the streets and out of abandoned houses. They were really messed up — heroin addicts, gangsters, and convicts. Some of them slept in old, abandoned cars.

I went around to different churches and presented the needs we had in the program. I didn't know Pastor Robles was the one making all the speaking arrangements for me. Pastors and various people in the city started to hear about me because I was always preaching on street corners. Sometimes when we went to churches, they gave us an offering or food for the program. Even though they did this, it still wasn't enough to cover all the needs we had. Because I was still collecting $122 a week from unemployment, I gave it all to the center after giving my tithes to the church.

One day the guys were murmuring and complaining more than usual. The devil was trying hard to stop us from doing the work of God in that program. The guys were complaining there wasn't enough food to eat, which was true, but I kept telling them to pray for God to provide the food. Instead, all they did was complain. Becoming frustrated with them, I told all five of them to leave the program. They didn't have to be there. I reminded them where they came from before we brought them into the program, living in abandoned houses and old cars. Back then, they often went without a meal for two or three days at a time, and now they were complaining about food. They had a good breakfast, and then they complained because they didn't have lunch.

While I was talking to the guys, a man named Mike knocked on the door; I opened it, and he walked in crying, saying that he needed help. Mike wanted to come to the center, so we took him in. After awhile, he told me he had a

186

paycheck he had to pick up. He also told me he wanted to donate the entire check to the center. When we heard that, we became excited! We knew God had made a way for us to get all the food we needed.

While I was in the program helping out, I learned so many things. I remember a young man named Raymond who joined the program. I had some brand new tailor-made pants, and Raymond didn't have any clothes at all. The Lord told me to give them to him; the following day he left the program. I was angry because he left after I gave him the pants; the Lord, however, told me I didn't give him any thing. The Lord had given them to him. I learned that when I gave something to people God really gave it to them because I couldn't give anyone anything.

The Lord began to bless me. I saw the way He provided for me because of the sacrifice I made by giving up everything I had. I gave up the apartment and my job to go there to work with these guys. I was never in want; I always had more than enough. My parents were happy for me, and they helped me in many ways too.

Bible College

One Sunday morning I woke up with a very strong desire to go to Bible college. I wanted to learn more about the Lord. I was teaching the guys in the program to pray. Some of them would, and some wouldn't. The desire grew stronger each day to leave everything and go to Bible college. But how could I go to Bible college when I had four outstanding debts? That morning I woke up thinking about Puerto Rico. I hadn't been there for ten years, not since 1970. I wanted to see my grandmother before she passed away. The Lord was already putting a desire in my heart to go there; He was revealing his perfect will for me, but I didn't completely understand it.

I went to church that morning with the guys from the program. During Sunday school, Pastor came and took me out to talk to me.

He said, "Luis Rolon tells me you have a desire to go to Bible college. There are three other young people in this church who have the same desire. We want to send someone to Bible college, but we have a problem. All three of these young people have been in the church longer than you have; they practically grew up here. However, I informed the board you are the one that we should send to the school, and Luis Rolon agreed with me. Even though they have been here longer than you have, they haven't done as much work as you have to bring people into the kingdom.

"We feel we need to prepare you because we know you are going to be an even bigger blessing to this church in the future. As it is, you've only been here a year, and this church has grown tremendously since the Lord brought you to be with us. I believe if we prepare you for the ministry to which God has called you, it will grow even more. We finally agreed on selecting you for Bible college, and we are going to take care of all your expenses."

I asked him where I was going to study; he told me I was going to Puerto Rico.

"Pastor," I said, "You know I don't understand Spanish that well."

He replied, "Joey, the Lord told me to send you to Puerto Rico, and if He told me to do that, then He will teach you. When you go, you will be representing this church. You let everyone know you have a church in Philadelphia that is supporting you. You go, and God will help you."

That afternoon I dropped the guys off at the center, and the other staff stayed with them. I went to my mother's house. When I saw her, I said, "Mom, the pastor in my church is sending me to Bible college in Puerto Rico, and they're going to pay everything for me to go."

She asked, "How in the world are you going to go if you have so many outstanding debts, and your car isn't paid off yet? How can you leave these bills behind?"

She was so discouraging that the anger I used to feel toward her began to rise up again. I left her and went to church that night. I asked them to pray for me.

Two days later I called my father and told him I needed to talk with him. I explained to him, "Pop, my church is paying for me to go to Bible college in Puerto Rico, but I'm going to need a plane ticket; I wanted to know if you could buy it for me."

My father said, "Call me tomorrow. I'll see what I can do."

I replied, "Pop, I have another problem. I owe four debts I have to pay before I leave. One is my car; if you want, you can keep it. Five payments are left, and you could continue to make them." He agreed, took the car, and made the payments.

About a week later I went to visit my mother, who told me, "Joey, I'm going to pay the bill you owe to Levin's for you so that you can go to Bible college." I was puzzled because of her change of heart. That night I dreamed I was on a bus going back to my job because they owed me some vacation money.

The next day I went back to Cardo's, just as I had done it in the dream, to find out if it was true. When I arrived, I found out they owed me about five hundred dollars. I took this money, paid off the other two debts I had, and gave some money toward the bill my mother was going to pay.

Then my father called me and told me he had already paid for my plane ticket; all I had to do was put the date on it! I continued to pray that the Lord would put everything together for me to go to Bible college. This was all new for me. I didn't know where I was going and what things would be like once I was there. I decided to fast and pray because I was somewhat nervous. I didn't know how I would survive there; I didn't speak Spanish that well.

I told Pastor that my father had paid for the plane ticket. That day at church an offering was taken up for me, and I was presented with a check for the tuition and told the date I would leave. I packed up everything and told Brother Robles I would see him when I came back that summer to help him.

At the airport I prayed, "God, if this is not Your perfect will for me to go to Puerto Rico, please don't let this plane take off. But if it is Your will, let me feel Your presence right now, and go before me because I am going to need You, Lord!"

After I prayed, I felt the presence of God, and I heard a voice in my heart say, "Do not fear, for I am with you. Do not be dismayed, for I am your God. I will strengthen you and help you, and I will uphold you with My righteous right hand." When I heard that, I knew the Lord was giving me the okay to go!

Chapter 23

Testing My Faith

I arrived in Puerto Rico August 19, 1980. Despite the sense of God's presence as the plane left Philadelphia and the assurance I was in His perfect will, my time of trial and testing was just about to begin.

After reaching the Luis Muñoz Marin Airport in San Juan, Puerto Rico, I sat there waiting for four and a half hours because whoever was supposed to pick me up wasn't there to meet me. However, I had the school's address and phone number, so I called to let them know I had arrived — and I was waiting to be picked up! I called a total of four times, but no one came to get me. I had been in Puerto Rico less than a day — less than half a day — but I was already frustrated and completely fed up with the whole thing.

Finally, I walked outside only to have three or four taxi drivers approach me, each one telling me if I paid him $50, he would drive me to the Assembly of God Bible College in Santa Monica, Bayamon, Puerto Rico. It was only a $5 fare, and here they were, trying to charge me all that extra money. And they didn't go away. They kept watching me as I waited. And waited. Those taxi drivers could tell I was just about to become unglued, but they kept bugging me about riding with one of them. By this time, I was so upset I almost punched a couple of them out! Even though I was saved, I still had plenty to learn and a lot of junk from my past I needed to let go.

Manny

While I was busy arguing with the taxi drivers, a man with tattoos on his arms walked up to me. He was wearing a T-shirt, a pair of old jeans spotted with paint, and a hat turned around backwards. To my surprise, he asked me if I was Joey Perez. When I replied that I was, he told me to follow him. Since I had no idea who *he* was, I just stood there and looked at him.

"Who are you?" I demanded. "Are you just going to come up to me and tell me to follow you? I don't even know who you are!"

As far as I was concerned, he looked just like a cold-blooded gangster — the kind I'd known back in Philly. Introducing himself, he replied, "My name is Manny Gonzalez, and I'm from the Bible College. I'm here to pick you up." He pointed to a van, and I saw the name of the school on it.

"Come on, Joey! Don't let my appearance fool you. The reason you see me looking like this is that we're doing a lot of painting at the school."

As we walked to the van, he commented, "You know, you came at a good time because you're going to be doing some of the painting too."

I told him I didn't mind at all because I had worked with the other guys from Temple Sinai Assembly of God back in Philadelphia to paint the entire front of our church, and we had even painted the inside too. As we climbed into the van, I mentioned to Manny I was hungry. In fact, I asked him if he liked chicken since that was what I was hungry for. He replied he also loved chicken, and we stopped at a "Golden Skillet," a chicken restaurant, on our way to the Bible College. As we pulled in, Manny pointed out a Teen Challenge Men's Rehabilitation Center right down the street, where he had done drug rehab and had gotten saved.

Once we had finished eating, Manny took me over to the Teen Challenge Center and gave me a tour of the place. He told me he had been born and raised in New York City, and he hardly understood any Spanish.

"I guess that makes two of us," I remarked, "because I have the same problem. Manny, I don't understand

Spanish, I don't know how to read it or write it, but I *do* know this is where the Lord has sent me."

Manny began to tell me that before he was saved, he had been a heroin addict for 25 years and had spent thirteen years in the penitentiary in New York. Like me, he had stabbed and even shot people. As he shared his life story with me, he told me that when he was in prison in New York, he used to take the bodies no one had claimed to the graveyard called "Potter's Field," a public burial ground for poor and unidentified people.

In turn, I shared some of my testimony with him. Starting that day, Manny and I became close friends even though he was roughly 42 years old, and I was only 23 at the time.

A Whole New World

Finally, I arrived at the Bible College. I had flown to Puerto Rico all "decked out" in my best clothes—a tailor-made suit, a designer shirt, and a pair of very expensive shoes. I had dressed that way with no idea I would soon have to change clothes in order to help paint the school! As we entered a building, my first stop was the office of the school's director, Carlos Osorio. He spent some time interviewing me, and then I handed him the check my church had given me to pay my tuition. Next, I filled out some forms and was shown to my dorm room. For some reason I had thought I was going to be in a room by myself. I soon found out, however, that I would be sharing "my" room with several other young men, some from the island of Puerto Rico and some from the United States.

I introduced myself to the others — Rolando Rojas from Mexico, Juan Cruz from Connecticut, and two guys named Javier and Angel. After we talked for a bit, I changed my clothes and went outside to help with the painting. As I

193

walked out of the building, I saw someone I already knew, a girl named Crucita Rivera. I had met her back in the States through a brother in Christ, Angel Robles — she was a member of his church in Lansdale, Pennsylvania. Crucita was a wonderful, committed sister in the Lord, and could she ever sing! God really used her to minister to people through her music.

As soon as I saw Crucita, I ran over and gave her a big hug. It felt so good to see a familiar face. However, when I looked into her eyes, I knew I had done something wrong. I wasn't aware the school was very strict in its policies regarding contact between men and women. Crucita explained that I wasn't supposed to hug or even talk with the girls at the Bible college. In shock, I protested that she was my *friend*, and I already knew her from Philadelphia! I had no idea that attitudes on my part just like this one were going to get me into a world of trouble at the Bible college. Apparently, I still needed God to break and mold me into the man He wanted me to be.

After I had been in school just a month or two, I was already up to my neck in problems. I attended my classes faithfully, but I couldn't understand anything being taught. Everything was taught in Spanish. After the first month, my teachers gave up on me. They didn't want to teach me anymore! Each of them went to the director's office, asking why my church in Philadelphia had sent me to a Bible college in Puerto Rico when they knew I didn't even speak the language. The director's response was to get me the textbooks in English. Then he found out I didn't understand English that well either. I could read it, but my comprehension was so poor I couldn't fully understand what I was reading. I was so discouraged and upset that I began to annoy the other students just to get some attention because I was being completely ignored by my teachers. Once I tied a girl's long hair to her chair, and when she stood up — well, you can be sure I got plenty of attention for that! My attitude was that if I wasn't going to learn anything in class, no one else was going to either.

Susie Santiago, one of the teachers, came to speak with me one day. Although she was from Puerto Rico and taught Spanish, she also spoke very good English.

"Joey, I'll make a deal with you. Since I am already here on campus every day, if you will give me an hour of your time daily, I'll teach you Spanish. But it has to be on your time and mine — not during the regular school hours. If you're willing to do that and you really want to learn Spanish, I'll help you."

As I looked at her, tears ran from my eyes. I didn't know how to receive a generous offer of assistance like that; before I was saved, no one had ever tried to help me in my entire life. I had a really low self-image. Even though I pretended to be tough, I struggled with a serious "inferiority complex" inside. On top of that, anger and resentment over the way people had treated me in the past still filled my heart.

Early Will I Seek You

Despite my many problems, I accepted Susie's help and told her I would meet her every afternoon at 4:00 so she could teach me. She began to work with me, and I really dedicated myself to my studies. One day I mentioned to her that ever since I had come to school, I had been waking up at 4:00 in the morning.

"Susie, I just can't go back to sleep. I toss and turn, and then I get up in time to pray for about 45 minutes before the day begins."

"Joey, I believe the reason you can't sleep is because the Holy Spirit wants you to get up early so you can pray more."

I took her words to heart. The next morning when I couldn't sleep, I got up and began to pray. Every morning I would be up and dressed right around 4:40 a.m., and I'd head for the chapel to pray for nearly two and a half hours. As the other guys — including Manny — realized I was doing this, they began to join me in the chapel. The next thing I knew, there were at least 16 of us going to the chapel every morning at 5:00 a.m. to pray.

However, there were these two guys at the school — the kind you meet wherever you go — who began to mock me every time they saw me get up early to pray. They even started placing bets as to how long I would last praying that early, making fun of me and the other guys too. In spite of their opposition, God gave me the strength to continue. By the end of September I began to feel a strong burden on my heart from the Lord to conduct a youth rally. I had been introduced to an Assembly of God Church in Royal Town, Bayamon, Puerto Rico that had a large group of young people. I shared with the pastor of that church the burden I had on my heart, and he was immediately excited about it. He already knew about me because he had heard me share my testimony in another church. This pastor, Julian Garilla, told me his church was already planning to conduct a big crusade, and he wanted me to preach the final night in the youth rally.

Anointed to Preach

Jesus used that rally to open more doors for me to share my testimony. Many of the pastors who attended that night invited me to come preach in their churches and hold street meetings. I began to preach on the streets all over Puerto Rico and realized what I really wanted was to go into the very worst communities on the island to hold these meetings. Not long after I met a music group, the

196

"Revelation Orchestra," directed by Eliezer Espinosa. Eliezer was a former heroin addict who had been saved for quite some time. He had a burden to minister in the streets and told me, whenever I was holding street meetings, he would like to come and back me up with music. I was glad to hear that. I knew we could team up and work together for the glory of God. Every time I had a day free from school, I'd set up a street meeting, and Eliezer and the "Revelation Orchestra" would minister to the people along with me. We became very close friends, and I told him I wanted to bring him to Philadelphia. Together, we started to plan a trip to do a number of street meetings in my hometown, in New York City, and in New Jersey.

All on Your Own

As I finished my first year of Bible College in 1981, I planned to go home to Philadelphia and begin to put together a crusade with Eliezer for the following year. I decided to give cassettes of Eliezer and his group to the churches I was going to work with in Philadelphia that summer. However, before I left Puerto Rico, I was surprised to learn that during my first year of school, I had passed all of my classes, except Spanish, with a "B" average. Even better than that, many of my teachers complimented me, telling me I was very intelligent. I couldn't imagine why they would say that; I felt all I had done was create problems in class because I couldn't understand half of what was being said!

My teachers, however, explained that they thought I really *was* intelligent; every time they gave me an assignment, I finished it. I told them I was sure they had given me "B" grades just because they felt sorry for me. Their response was, "NO! You did the work you were supposed to do and earned your grades all on your own."

God used their words to help heal the low self-esteem that had bothered me my whole life.

Trying to understand the class work taught in Spanish wasn't the only difficulty I had faced my first year at the Assembly of God Bible School. On different occasions we didn't have much food in the college. I remember once we had to eat sausages and corn for three weeks in a row. We also ate bananas from the banana trees growing on the campus grounds. In fact, we ate bananas in every possible way you could imagine! The school ran on donations given by churches; sometimes, the money simply wasn't there. Still, despite my difficulties with the language and the food problem, my first year there had also been a time of blessing as I watched God work through my life for His glory.

Tragedy and Sorrow

I arrived home in Philadelphia for the summer right around June 1, 1981. Just ten days after my arrival, our family experienced a tragedy that almost shattered us. My father had been having problems with some men right around the corner from where he lived. There was a particular guy who had "taken a liking" to one of the daughters of my father's girlfriend. She had made it clear she wasn't interested. This man wasn't taking the rejection too well, and as a result, he was beginning to cause trouble for my father.

That afternoon my brother Willie and I had been helping one of our relatives move. As I drove the U-Haul truck down the street, we saw our father on the corner of 3rd and Cambria. We stopped to talk with him, and he told us about the trouble with the neighbor. Willie got out of the truck to go home with him, and I drove on. Margaret, my father's German-Irish girlfriend, was at the house along with her daughter, Barbara, and another daughter, also named

Margaret. My father's girlfriend loved Willie as if he was her own son, and in return, my brother was very close to Margaret.

They had all been drinking, and Willie joined in with them until everyone there was almost completely drunk. My father had some loaded guns at the house because of the trouble with the neighbor, and he had given one to Willie that day. My brother began to clown around, pointing the gun at my father's girlfriend and pretending he was going to shoot her. Margaret told him to stop it. Willie unloaded the bullets from the revolver so there would be no possibility of an accident, but he was too drunk to realize he had taken only five of the six bullets out. One was still left in the barrel and Willie had no idea it was there.

"I'm gonna *kill* you, Margaret," Willie joked as he pointed the gun at her again. Once more, she told him to knock it off. To show her the gun wasn't dangerous, Willie put it to his own head, cocked it, and pulled the trigger. It just made a "click"; the chamber was empty. He did it a second time. Once again, another empty chamber clicked harmlessly. Willie then pointed the gun at Margaret who was sitting five feet away on the couch, watching television with her feet propped up on a chair. He pulled the trigger.

The one remaining bullet killed Margaret instantly, splattering her blood on the chair and the wall of the living room. Frantic with grief, my father called me, and I rushed over to his house, bringing Pastor Jose del Toro, Sister Catalina Rolon, and another woman from the church, Sister Isabella. I found my father weeping in anguish, and immediately, I sensed the presence of darkness in that place. I searched my father's house, finding nothing unusual until I entered his bedroom. Behind the door I saw candles lit to seven idols — false gods. My father was practicing witchcraft — against other people!

I began to command those evil spirits to stop their work in the name of Jesus, using the authority He gave to

199

believers. I asked my father if we could pray for him. He said yes, and after praying, I left. A woman many people loved was dead. My father's heart was broken. And my brother Willie sat in jail waiting to be charged with her death.

Trouble at Home

When I had first returned to Philadelphia that summer, I had lived with my mother and sister Wandy but I tried not to stay around the house too much. My other brothers and sisters gave my mother's common-law husband such a hard time that there was no peace in the house. The devil used this situation to discourage me even more. Finally, just two weeks after I had arrived, my mother told me she was moving to Puerto Rico so she and her husband could live together without all that strife. Once they left, I moved in with my sister Evelyn who lived at 265 W. Westmoreland Street, just down from where my mother had lived.

When I moved in with my sister, however, I found her house was even more filled with conflict than my mother's had been. People cursed at each other constantly, day and night. Evelyn's girlfriends were always dropping by the house, flirting with me and trying to entice me into sin. She hardly had any food in the house so I tried to make sure the refrigerator and the cupboards had something to eat in them. The whole situation at her house was completely crazy! Evelyn continually fought with her husband, even beating him up on occasion. Her children cursed at her and at each other. Even the neighbors fought with each other all the time.

Preaching His Word

Despite the sorrow and turmoil in our family, I still looked forward to helping Brother Angel Robles once more with the men's rehabilitation center. To my disappointment I found out he was turning the Center over to a Mennonite Church. He simply couldn't support it any longer—he didn't have any financial help from local churches. He was so discouraged that he gave the Center away to Liberty Ministries, run by Glen Alderfer. Glen held street meetings right around the corner from the Center, and John Roman, a brother in the Lord who knew me, asked him if I could share my testimony. Glen agreed, and I preached for about 25 minutes out on the streets.

When I gave the altar call, God moved on people's hearts, and about 30 were saved. Glen was excited that night because so many people had come to know the Lord. That night he had brought a few of his friends to the street meeting, including Deacon Jake Proctor and his wife Hazel. They were a beautiful black couple in their mid-sixties and members of Zion Baptist Church. They heard what God had done in my life, and as a result, He gave them such a great love for me that I couldn't comprehend it. They constantly tried to help me grow more in the Lord, inviting me to come to the street meetings they held with their ministry, "Crusaders for Christ." I was more than happy to receive that invitation because I wanted to get involved in whatever God was doing! In addition to my own church's street meetings, I helped Deacon Proctor with his meetings and began to experience some very unusual responses to my ministry.

Sometimes as I preached, people would yell at me to shut up — they didn't want to hear what I had to say. When we first began the meetings in my old neighborhood, people would curse at us, telling our team to get off their corner. Others threatened to kill me. However, I noticed that even though I was receiving such serious threats, no one could get near enough to harm me because the Holy Spirit's power wouldn't let them get that close.

When Deacon Proctor first took me to the old neighborhoods where I used to gang-war, people there didn't recognize me because I looked like a different man from the one they had known. I had shaved off my beard. I combed my hair differently. I had also lost weight because of the fasting I had been doing back in Puerto Rico. As they heard my testimony, however, they realized right away who I was. They stayed silent in the meeting as they tried to figure out just what had happened to me. Some of these people received the Lord, saying, "If God can change you, He can do the same for me!" As I prayed and laid hands on those who had gotten saved, demons often came out of them, screaming as they departed. We also saw God heal many sick people by His mighty power.

That summer I began to help John Roman with his drug rehabilitation program. He even wanted me to move into his Center to work with him. However, I began to get the feeling there might be some jealousy developing; the guys in his program were getting closer to me, seeking me out for counseling. I decided it was time for me to move on because I didn't want any conflicts with a brother in Christ.

I began to wonder what else the Lord had for me to do as I continued to work with my church. After all, I had told my fellow church members I didn't want to just sit around doing nothing the whole summer! I wanted to keep working for God's kingdom. He honored that desire. We held a street meeting right in the heart of my old neighborhood — 4th and Indiana Streets. When we arrived to conduct the meeting, there were people inside the corner bar and about a hundred more hanging around outside getting high. We started by singing a couple of songs, and then the meeting was turned over to me. I began to preach, telling the people gathered there that God wanted to set them free—and He had the power to do it.

Signs and Wonders Follow

Suddenly, this guy came out of the corner bar with a hook knife — a knife with a curved "hook" used to cut rope or heavy cord — in his hand. He ran across the street, coming right for me. When some of the other guys on the corner saw him, they ran up to him, put a gun to his head and held knives at his throat and his stomach, telling him, "If you touch that preacher, we'll kill you!" When the other brothers from my church who had come with me saw this, they were amazed. I had already experienced attacks like this in Puerto Rico, and God had protected me every single time. I had seen the power of God shield His children from harm.

That night I was just waiting for this man to get close to me. I wanted to lay hands on him in the name of Jesus and drive out that violent spirit within him. As it turned out, I didn't even have to do that. God used those guys on the corner to protect me. I actually had to call out to them to leave him alone and not hurt him, "Just let him go!" Those guys asked that man if he even knew who I was. When he said he didn't, they told him, "Listen, he used to be our gang leader!" and then pulled him away from me. Later, when I gave the altar call, that same guy — the one who had tried to come after me with the hook knife — was the very first person to get saved.

Philip and Edwin

One evening, I helped Deacon Proctor conduct a street meeting at 33rd and Cumberland Streets. Roughly 40 people were saved that night, and the power of God moved strongly to set people free from drug addiction. I went back to Evelyn's afterward so filled with joy — just happy all over because people had come to the Lord. After I got home, I had just sat down to relax before going to bed when I heard all this noise coming from the corner. People were screaming, and my sister Evelyn ran out there screaming too. I hurried down to the corner to find out what was happening, and when I got there, I saw my two brothers, Philip and Edwin, fighting each other. They were both drunk. This was another reason my mother had moved to Puerto Rico — the anger between my brothers.

When I saw my brothers fighting, I moved nearer to them only to see Philip pull out a large knife. He raised it up high in the air, ready to stab Edwin in the neck. I knew if that knife entered Edwin's body, he'd be dead. To this day, I don't how I did it, but when I saw that knife coming down, I grabbed Philip's arm — the one with the knife — and threw both of my brothers to the ground. People thought I was crazy, jumping into a fight like that. Edwin got up from the ground first. When he saw me, he didn't say anything; he had always respected me. However, when Philip got to his feet, he looked at me and screamed, "I'll kill you!" and grabbed the knife again. As he came toward me, I yelled, "In the name of Jesus, you're not killing anyone. *In the name of Jesus!*"

My voice was so loud that when I looked around, everyone had become silent; it was as if some kind of peace had come upon them. I looked around at Philip and said, "That's right, there is power in the blood of Jesus! You with your knife — you don't scare me." I walked over to him, took the knife out of his hand, and threw it up onto the roof. Then I looked at the crowd.

"You know what you all need? *You need Jesus!*"

I walked away crying because I realized how close Philip had come to killing his own brother. Back at Evelyn's, I went to my room and continued to weep because it hurt to see the condition my family was still in. I prayed God would work a miracle in their lives. Later after all that had happened out on the corner, I heard that my brothers hugged and kissed each other, saying how much they loved each other. But then they went right back to their drinking.

Time to Leave

I began praying to God, asking Him to take me out of Philadelphia.

"Lord, if I stay here any longer," I told Him, "I'm not going to make it!"

By this time, I had been saved for slightly over 2 years, and I was feeling weak spiritually. I knew if I remained in Philadelphia much longer, I was going to fall into sin. I was facing temptation: women coming onto me and many of my friends from the past offering me drugs. I saw all the money they were making as drug dealers, and I remembered how well-off financially I had once been doing the same thing. But now I was almost broke — I hardly had any money. When I went to the unemployment office, I learned I could only collect six more checks.

I went to my father, asking if he would buy my plane ticket so I could return to Puerto Rico. He told me he would, adding that as long as I was in Bible College, he'd buy me round-trip plane tickets. I also asked him to lend me some money. I wanted to buy sound equipment so I could preach in the streets, and I also needed a car to travel around Puerto Rico from meeting to meeting. My father lent me the money and a few days later, he called to tell me I didn't have to pay him back. Just after he lent me the money, he won big on the lottery. He figured it was God blessing him for helping me. However, I knew it wasn't God letting him win the lottery! He was being deceived by the devil to keep on gambling; every time he gave me money, he would play the lottery and win. My father was also heavily involved in idol worship. He had somewhere between 10 and 15 figures of saints in his house with candles constantly lit to them. Every time I went over there, I came away with a terrible headache and an agitated mind. Just for that reason, I didn't like to go visit him.

Chapter 24

New Burden, Fresh Anointing

When my father bought me the plane ticket, I left Philadelphia. It was time for me to get out, and coming back to Puerto Rico was like being in heaven! This time I decided to live off-campus and commute to the Bible College. This would give me more freedom to conduct street meetings at night after I had attended school during the day. Upon my return I met an older married couple, Luis and Teresa Maldonado. Luis's father had once been the superintendent of police on the island of Puerto Rico. They told me I could live at their house, which I did for about two months. They treated me just like a son.

I began to help them out at the pizzeria they owned. Sometimes they'd give me money in return for my help, but I really didn't want it. I just enjoyed the opportunity to serve them, and I was grateful to them for letting me live at their house. They lent me their car whenever I needed it to go to my preaching engagements, and they helped me in any way they could. They were a gift from God — the father and mother I always wished I had. They showed me love — the love I wanted from my own mother, but which she was not able to give. Everywhere I went with them, people thought I really was their son. Their relatives even began to treat me as part of the family. Teresa Maldonado had a brother-in-law named Toin who was the pastor of a church in Bayamon, all the way up in the mountains. He frequently took me there with him, and I loved it. It was a wonderful place to pray. As I was praying in their prayer room one particular time, a brother from the church came up and tapped me on the shoulder.

"Joey, go to the altar because there is a great blessing for you from the Lord."

At that time I felt spiritually weak and just "drained out." I didn't feel "right." When I got to the altar, God's power fell upon me like I had never felt it before. I began praying, and my body started trembling. I was speaking in tongues, praying very loudly, and all of a sudden everyone else joined with me in prayer. God's power came into that place in a mighty way. I also felt as if a fresh anointing from God was being restored to my life that day.

Made in Heaven

As I started my second year of Bible College, I realized to my regret that Manny wasn't coming back. We had grown very close my first year of school. First year students weren't allowed to leave campus from Monday through Friday, but sometimes Manny would sneak out to get some chicken for us. I knew I would miss him very much. He had been offered an opportunity to run a ministry called "New Life for Girls," and he decided to accept the offer. I told Manny I thought it was going to be a difficult experience for him. After all, he was a single man going to work in a women's home where a number of girls were getting off drugs. But he did it. He was able to walk in purity there until God gave him a wife — a real testimony to God's power to keep us out of sin.

Now that I was back in Puerto Rico, I resumed the street meetings with Eliezer Espinosa and his orchestra. After I finished the school day, I'd go to Eliezer's house, and we'd leave to conduct meetings along with the "Revelation Orchestra." His people liked having me around, and I felt we were a team "made in heaven." Eliezer's orchestra sang "Christian salsa" — and some of the more "legalistic" churches just didn't like it, criticizing him for being worldly. Since I worked with him preaching in the meetings, I was highly criticized too, even though so many people were getting saved. Unfortunately, some of these churches that had such a narrow view of what was "acceptable" were too busy condemning us to see God's hand moving upon the lives of people who needed Him.

I went to stay with my uncle who lived in the Canteras area of Santurce, Puerto Rico — one of the worst communities on that side of the island. Even the police didn't like going in there; whenever they had to come into that area, they made sure they entered in groups of four or five. Every day as I came home from school, I saw junkies hanging out on the corners. These guys looked "like hell"; they *really* needed the Lord in their lives.

My Friend "Ralph"

I was riding the bus to my uncle's house from school one day, and I noticed a homeless man. He tried to sneak onto the bus from the side door, but the bus driver saw him and stopped the bus to make him get off. I was seated all the way at the back, watching what was going on. This man had been trying to find a place to sit, but people cursed at him and pushed him away every time he attempted to sit down. The bus driver was ready to put him off when I stood up and said, "Leave him alone. I'll pay his fare."

I paid his fare of twenty-five cents and told him to sit with me. Everyone on the bus stared at me because I was all dressed up, wearing a tie and carrying a briefcase under my arm. They couldn't understand what I was doing because this guy was so dirty. His pants and shirt were ripped, and the soles of his bare feet were black with grime from the streets. His hands were dirty, he looked like he hadn't shaved in months, he had long filthy hair, and he smelled terrible too.

After I paid his fare, I heard people in the back of the bus saying, "Don't bring him back here!" So we sat in the front of the bus, and I put my arm around him as if he were an old friend of mine. I realized God was giving me a great opportunity to witness to all these people — and to this man.

I said to him, "How are you doing, Ralph?"

He looked at me in surprise because I had just given him that name — I had no idea what his name was. I was just trying to get a message across to the other people on the bus. I kept talking.

"How are you doing, Ralph? You don't look too good. What happened? You know, Ralph, you have to take a bath, comb your hair, and shave. That's why nobody here wanted you next to them. But you know me — I've known you for a long time." (I didn't know him *at all*.)

He kept staring at me, and I continued, "Ralph, I used to be just like you. As a matter of fact, every time I got on the bus, everyone would shut up because if they didn't give me their money, I took it from them. Lots of people didn't want me around because of the kind of person I was.

"Hey, Ralph, you know what I used to be — I was a drug dealer, a gang leader, and an addict! You know I was always going around sticking people up. I was rejected just like you.

"But you know, Ralph, thank God for Jesus Christ! Even though these people don't like you, Jesus loves you — and I like you! You're my friend, no matter what. You'll always be my friend, and I'll pay your way on the bus anytime I see you."

As I was talking to him, there was complete silence throughout the bus. The other people kept quiet, listening to every word I was saying. I told Ralph he needed the Lord. Jesus was the only one who had ever changed me, and He could change him too. When I got to my stop, I turned to "Ralph" and said, "Come on, let's go! You're taking a bath in my house and changing your clothes."

As we got off the bus, I started to pray — really hard. My uncle wasn't a Christian, although my aunt and cousins went to a Seventh Day Adventist Church in Barrio Obrero in

Santurce. My uncle had a small grocery store around the corner from his house. I was praying God would touch my uncle's heart because I had promised this guy he could come take a bath at my house. I also wanted to bless him with some new clothes. I didn't know what my uncle was going to do; he might not let him take a bath — he might not even let him *in* the house!

As we got closer to my neighborhood, people began watching us. Here was this filthy guy, no shoes or socks, feet black with dirt. He looked horrible, but every time I looked into his eyes, I could see how lonely he was. My heart went out to him because I knew Jesus could do a new work in his life and change him.

Not a Bum!

When we got to my uncle's store, he was standing at his door talking with a couple of his friends. Meanwhile, the junkies standing on the corner started yelling, making fun of Ralph.

"Hey, Joey, where'd you find that bum at?"

"You shut up! He's my friend. You don't call any of my friend's bums. *He's not a bum.*"

I made the introductions saying, "Uncle, this is my friend, Ralph (I still didn't know his real name)."

My uncle just looked at him. I continued, "I found him on the bus, and everyone was pushing him away. He's been having a real bad time, so I just wanted to know — is there a possibility he could take a bath at home?"

Before my uncle could respond, I said, "I'll buy the razor blades and the soap. I'll clean up everything afterward too."

After studying Ralph for a moment, my uncle gave me the okay, and I took Ralph inside. Before getting into the shower, he took off his clothes. They were so dirty, the flies

211

began gathering around them! They were really stinking, so I threw everything away. I took those old clothes, put them in a double bag, and threw them in the trash. Then I got him some of my own clothes — some underwear, socks, pants, and a shirt. My uncle had closed his store and come into the house. He wasn't even a Christian, but he got a pair of shoes and a couple more pairs of pants to give Ralph.

When Ralph got out of the shower, he looked *and smelled* clean. He had shaved, and I hardly recognized him. He looked "brand new." After he dressed and combed his hair, I put the extra clothes we had gathered into a bag. We went outside together, and the guys on the corner didn't recognize him.

"Hey, Joe! Where's that guy you had with you?"

"You can't tell? Here he is, right here!"

Taking a second look at him, all they could say was, "Wow! What a little soap and water can do!"

I walked with Ralph as we headed back to the bus stop. On the way, I bought him some chicken and a baked potato to eat, and he began to tell me what had happened to him. He had been a general contractor who had owned his own business, but somehow things started to go wrong. He lost everything he had, and he wasn't making enough money to pay his bills. He went bankrupt, and his wife became so upset and angry she left him and cut off all contact between him and his children. Here was a successful businessman who because of the pressure of unexpected events, went downhill and began to live on the streets. I was surprised a man who'd had so much could become homeless.

After he finished eating, I gave him some money — about $3.25.

"Ralph, whatever you do, don't try to sneak back on the bus. Pay your way this time."

"I look so clean! If I go back to my neighborhood, they're going to think I hit the lottery or something. Who knows? They'll probably beat me because they think I have money on me."

I told him not to go back to his old neighborhood but to find a good gospel-preaching church where he could give his heart to Jesus Christ. I prayed with him, and he left. The way he looked at me, I know he was touched by God's love and power. Someday I hope to see this man again in Puerto Rico, serving the Lord and doing well. Even to this day, I don't know his real name.

God used what I did for Ralph to create a burden on my heart to help people on the streets. I set up a meeting with the director of Teen Challenge in Puerto Rico because I wanted to share with him my desire to help the homeless. I needed his counsel, but he didn't seem to know how to advise me. As we talked, I became downcast and walked out of his office feeling disheartened. I went home, thinking there was no way I could ever help people like "Ralph," but that burden was already on my heart to minister to them. Little did I know that by His mighty power, God would make my desire a reality.

Where Sin Abounds

I also had a desire in my heart to hold a street meeting in the Canteras area of Santurce where my uncle lived. It seemed like someone was always being attacked in that community and many people had already been killed there. One particular day, a man was shot four times in front of my uncle's house, falling dead right on my uncle's porch. On another occasion, I was sitting on the porch reading the newspaper. I watched a man get off his bike and walk into a house nearby. Suddenly, I heard four gunshots come from within the house. That same man came back outside, climbed onto his bike, and rode off as if nothing had happened. As it turned out, the man he shot didn't die — but he was paralyzed for life.

Yet another time, I was sitting on our porch talking to Papo, a friend from across the street who was also a brother in the Lord. Suddenly, I heard shouting, and when I looked over at my uncle's store, some guys had a man down on the ground. They were holding shotguns on him and taking his money. I was amazed they didn't kill him. These were young guys, drug addicts who hung out on the corner. They did this in broad daylight, and no one said anything at all. They didn't dare; they were afraid of what would happen to them.

When I saw this kind of attack in our neighborhood, I thought, "The time has come to do something!" I went to seven different churches in the community to ask for their support so I could hold street meetings there. Not one of them would help me. Many church members were shocked when they learned their own churches would not help us with the meetings. I had wanted to get the churches involved so the people who got saved at the meetings would have a place to grow in the Lord.

Help From the Unbelievers

My uncle knew the burden I had on my heart for these street meetings. I told him what had happened with the churches and explained I already had a group who would lead the music while I did the preaching. I just needed someone to supply the electricity for the sound equipment and help people who got saved find a church where they could receive a foundation in the Lord.

"Come with me," my uncle responded. "I know some people who live on the corner. If you want to hold a street meeting, I'm sure they'll supply the electricity."

When we went to that house, I realized the people who lived there were Christians. My uncle introduced me to them, told them I was his nephew, and explained that I wanted to hold a street meeting on the corner. He asked if they would let me run a line for the electricity to power our sound equipment. This brother in the Lord looked at me in surprise and said, "You can do all the street meetings you want, but I'll tell you right now that not even a fly will get saved!"

"Well, that's just fine," I responded in disgust, "because I'm not coming here to preach to flies but to people who are lost. They *will* get saved if you'll just let me use your electricity. You don't even have to come to the meetings if you don't want to!"

This brother's unbelief had just added to how downcast I felt. The churches didn't want to back me up, and now the Christians who lived in this drug-filled, crime-infested community wouldn't do anything to help people get saved. We left, and my uncle took me across the street to another house. When we got to this woman's house, I saw she had altars to all kinds of idols. She worshipped false gods and images of saints — in fact, she was a witch! In spite of that, I asked her if she would let me use her electricity to hold a street meeting where I would preach the gospel of Jesus Christ. She looked right at me and said, "Sure, you can plug in all your sound equipment!"

This baffled me. I had gone to the Body of Christ for help in holding evangelistic meetings, and they turned me down. I had gone to sinners, and they were more than willing to help me!

A Man Named Michael

Eliezer Espinosa joined us with his orchestra. A girl named Lucy and her sister came out to help, along with Papo and his wife Ana. There were only six of us, not including the orchestra, who were planning to brave a whole community plagued with drugs and crime.

The first night of the meeting when the orchestra started playing, people began to stream in from everywhere. About 400 people attended that night. This was such a compact community that people had to sit on porches, on their cars, and even on the roofs of houses. Everywhere I looked, I saw a sea of faces. After the orchestra sang several songs and shared some of their testimonies, I felt in my heart it was time to preach and asked Eliezer to turn the service over to me. I preached for only 20 minutes, and then I gave the altar call.

As I was inviting the people to come forward and be saved, the Holy Spirit gave me the name of a man who was there and insight into his situation. Although I didn't know who he was, I obeyed the Spirit's prompting in my heart, announcing "There is a young man here tonight whose name is Michael. The Holy Spirit showed me some people have a contract out on your life. They want to kill you. If you don't repent tonight, there's not going to be a tomorrow for you!"

No sooner were those words out of my mouth, than nine guys came forward, bringing "Michael" with them. He was trembling, partly from fear and partly because he knew that while I didn't know him, God did. As it turned out, I didn't know any of the people who were involved in crime in that community.

In front of the crowd, I asked him, "Do you know me?" He replied he didn't. I told him, "These people are looking to kill you, and they are on their way! You need to give your heart to Jesus tonight — He's the only one who can protect you."

Michael accepted Jesus that night as his Lord and Savior. Seeing what the Lord was doing, another 13 people came forward to give their lives to Him. As God's Spirit came upon people, many began to fall to the ground as if they had fainted — God's power was that strong and

216

overwhelming. One woman fell to the ground and began to writhe just like a snake, screaming and foaming at the mouth. In the name of Jesus, our team commanded the evil spirits within her to leave her. We saw the truth of the Bible demonstrated: God has given Christians the power to drive out evil spirits and to heal every kind of sickness in Jesus' name!

The second night of the meeting, 20 people got saved. On the third night, another 10 came to the Lord. God moved powerfully those three nights, and the churches that hadn't wanted to back me began coming to our meetings once they heard what was happening. On the last night of this street meeting, one particular pastor gave me an offering. I told him I didn't want it; I was still upset because the local churches hadn't been willing to be part of what God was doing in their own community. Now I was being given an offering. Instead of taking it, I gave this pastor the list of those who had been saved and asked him to follow up with them.

Favor From the Lord

At the same time God was saving people, He was using the meetings to introduce me to the community. By this time, people had learned who I was and what I was all about. A week after this crusade, a group of 10 guys were just standing out on the corner. One of them called me over, and when I went to shake his hand, he didn't want to touch me. He had seen God's power moving in the meetings as I laid hands upon people, and he was scared that if I touched him, he'd fall to the ground! However, he was willing to talk to me.

"You're a true man of God, and I know the Spirit of God is upon you. He's the one giving you revelation — He's showing you things only God Himself could know!"

This man's name was Yeyo, and he had been saved in one of our street meetings but wasn't really walking with the Lord. He continued, "We've been watching you for over a month. At first we thought you were a businessman, and you had money in that briefcase. You know, we were even thinking about sticking you up!

"Now we know you're a man of God. You confused us at first. We knew there was *something* about you because you have that "jitterbug" walk — you know, that little "stroll." In some ways, you looked like a businessman, but in other ways, you seemed like one of us.

"We know you used to live the same kind of life we're living now, and we just wanted to welcome you to our community. Whatever we can do to help, we'll be glad to do it."

When I heard that, I was really blessed to know these men felt this way about me. God was giving me favor even with the unsaved people in that community.

As I finished my second year of Bible College, I began to get homesick. I missed my family in Philadelphia. My sister Debbie's husband had just been killed. My sister Gigi was in bad shape too. Her husband shot a girl three times, killing her. Even here in Puerto Rico, my mother was still having problems. I wondered why God kept blessing *me*-giving me His grace and favor with so many people - but not bringing my family into His Kingdom. I think at this point, however, the problem lay with them and not with God. They were waiting to see whether or not I would continue to serve the Lord.

Chapter 25

God Expands His Work

When I came home for summer vacation after my second year of school, I brought Eliezer Espinosa and his group with me to conduct street meetings in Philadelphia. We began working with a number of churches, and God continued to bless our efforts! Whenever we held street meetings, people continued to get saved by the power of God. Many were set free from drug addiction and from various evil spirits. Others were healed from all kinds of diseases.

Some people, however, kept trying to get close to me and to the orchestra in order to harm us, but they couldn't come too near because God's power protected us. Others came to our services drunk, trying to disrupt the meetings, but we would lay hands on them and the Lord would cause them to become sober. It seemed wherever I went, the enemy tried to stop me, but the more he tried, the more determined I was to go forward in the name of Jesus to preach the gospel. I wanted to let people know God is the God of all, and He rules and reigns over this world. I was learning more about the Bible, and it caused me to minister with a strong desire to accomplish much for His kingdom. God's Word was a fire burning so powerfully in my heart that all I wanted to do was preach. Meanwhile, I kept praying for my family to be saved.

God Will Not Share His Glory

When I returned to Puerto Rico at the end of the summer, however, some problems came up, and I wasn't able to take classes at the Bible college that semester. Instead, I went to live with Raul Concepcion, a Christian brother who lived in Anasco on the west side of the island. I continued to do a number of street meetings, and God's ministry through me started to grow. I had opportunities to witness over the radio. When that happened, many other doors started to open for me to continue preaching the gospel. Churches began to call me, asking me to come and share my testimony.

One day, after speaking on a radio station, several people came to me, asking me to come to their area to preach the powerful Word of God. I was going so many places that I began to be fairly well known. Whenever I held a street meeting, at least 30 churches supported the effort. I had only been saved for three and a half years, but the Lord was using me tremendously. Unfortunately, pride was beginning to raise its ugly head in my life. I had begun to think I was God's "mighty man" and there was no one else on earth as valuable to God's work as I was. The Lord, however, was not about to let me continue on this path.

At one of my street meetings, I got up to share my testimony and suddenly began to tremble in fear so much I could hardly speak. In fact, I was able to speak for only a few minutes before I had to sit back down. On another occasion, the meeting was turned over to me, but I found my voice was completely gone! I was hardly able to whisper, and there was no way I could preach for 20 or 30 minutes. God allowed this to happen in order to break the pride in my heart and teach me that He would share His glory with no other. The great things happening through my ministry were not a result of my goodness or ability. They were a result of God's faithfulness to perform His Word. It was His grace and power working *through* me. Any good thing that took place — the lost getting saved, the sick being healed, the oppressed being set free — was God's work alone, and only He deserved the glory for it.

Emergency!

After three years on the island of Puerto Rico, I found I didn't want to go back to Philadelphia. Every time I went home, I became discouraged. After staying in Anasco with Raul for a few months, I decided to spend some time with Eliezer Espinosa in Bayamon. Eliezer and his orchestra had planned a missionary trip to the Dominican Republic, and they invited me to go with them. They were going to pay my way so I could go — roughly a $100 round trip. Even though I wanted to accompany them, I felt in my heart that for some reason I shouldn't. The morning they left, I was sitting in a rocking chair on Eliezer's porch when his sister-in-law came running out to tell me I had an important phone call from Philadelphia. I grabbed the phone, and my older sister Evelyn was crying on the other end of the line. Our brother Philip had been shot. He had even died on the operating table, but the doctors had brought him back to life. Now, however, they were only giving him another 24 hours to live. As I hung up, I began to weep thinking Philip was going to die without Jesus. I called my father to see if he would pay for my plane ticket. He did, and I returned to Philadelphia.

Upon my arrival I found out it was Dingo, my cousin Junito's "would be" father-in-law who had shot Philip. Junito had been fighting with Gloria, the woman he was living with, and Philip was there too. They were all drunk. Suddenly, Gloria's father Dingo pulled out a gun. Dingo was a good man who had never been a troublemaker of any kind. As he pulled out the gun, my brother saw it and pulled out a knife to stab Dingo. As Philip ran toward him, Dingo shot my brother. Philip had been about a foot away when he was shot in the chest; the bullet then ripped down through his intestines.

I was on my way to Dingo's house to find out exactly what had happened, but on my way, I found Gloria. I told her

221

to get into the car. People standing around on the corner thought I was going to hurt her; they didn't understand God had already made a dramatic change in my life. I knew Philip, unlike Dingo, *was* a big troublemaker, never minding his own business, frightening people, and even doing things like slicing up their faces. When I reached Dingo's house, I found him sobbing. Gloria's mother was there, and as I walked into the house, the family stood around outside. No one said a word to me.

I gave Gloria's mom a kiss on the cheek and asked her what had happened. As she began to explain, my own father arrived at the house. It turned out Dingo had shot my brother out of fear. He was right to be afraid; Philip had stabbed so many people that Dingo would have been just one more person my brother had hurt. I knew Dingo would not have harmed my brother intentionally — he wouldn't even hurt a fly. In fact, I had hurt people trying to *defend* Dingo because I really liked him. Whenever anyone gave him trouble, I took care of them. He was a good man.

A Chance for Philip

After I heard what had happened, I went to the hospital to see my brother. Philip had all kinds of tubes going into his stomach, nose, and arms. I tried to pray for him, but I was crying too much. Even the nurse in his room was speechless as tears ran down my face. In the past I would never have cried to see a person in Philip's condition. But God had changed my heart of stone to a heart of human flesh, and I could sense my brother's pain. My mother and sisters were there weeping. Although everyone at the hospital was waiting for the worst to happen, I felt faith rise in my heart. I went into Philip's room again and laid my hands on him in the name of Jesus. I asked the Lord that if He was going to take my brother, He would allow Philip to regain consciousness for a few hours so I could share the message of salvation with him.

The next day we received the news Philip was improving. He had been in critical condition, but now he was upgraded to stable condition. Everyone knew this was a true miracle from God. I went to my church to share what had happened. Some of the brothers and sisters went to the hospital to continue praying for my brother.

After a week in stable condition, the doctors had to rush him once again into emergency surgery because a blood vessel to his heart had ruptured. This time the doctors weren't giving him even twelve hours to live — but he survived. Philip had already died three times on the operating table, and each time the doctors had brought him back to life. During this period his wife came to church with me one Sunday and accepted the Lord. When Philip was once more in stable condition, I shared with him about Jesus, and he accepted Him that very day. About thirty days later, the doctors declared Philip was out of danger. I went back to Puerto Rico where I had a number of preaching engagements to fulfill.

After I had been back in Puerto Rico for about ten days, I received another phone call telling me Philip had died a fourth time, but once more the doctors had been able to revive him. I returned to Philadelphia again to pray for my brother, and through the kindness of God, he continued to live. I prayed constantly that God would have mercy upon Philip. I wanted to see him preaching alongside me one day. Two weeks later, on June 22nd, I flew back to Puerto Rico but *knew* it was time for me to return to Philadelphia for good. I wrote my brother Willie that I was moving home permanently, and I needed a place to stay. He told me to come live with him.

Back in Philly to Stay

Once I returned to Philadelphia, however, there was more trouble to deal with in my family. My sister Vivian's husband was in jail for shooting a police officer, and I stayed with her for a few weeks. After that, I went to live with Willie, but nothing seemed to be working out for me. I had sold all my sound equipment and left my car in Puerto Rico. I thank God that when I returned to Philadelphia, my father gave me another car. I took the money I had received for the sound equipment and invested it in some clothes. Then I sold those clothes so I could have money to travel around preaching God's Word. I spent about $900 on clothes and then made back around $3,000. I always knew how to make a living, but I also knew selling clothes wasn't really God's plan for me!

I had been home for around six months when I was in a car wreck in November of 1983. A driver hit me from behind, and I was thrown under another car. Nothing was going right. One day I was home with the television on, but I wasn't really watching it. Instead, I was thinking about everything going on in my life. At that moment, I received a phone call from Glen Alderfer. He told me he had a job for me if I was willing to work in Lansdale, Pennsylvania. However, right before he called me, while I was "watching" television, the Lord had given me a vision of a house on a hill. In the vision, I was living in that house.

After Glen told me about the job, I described the "house on the hill" and told him the Lord had shown me I was going to live there. Oh, did Glen become excited! He quickly asked me if Deacon Proctor had already spoken with me, and I told him no. He explained if I accepted the job, I would get to live in *the very house I had seen in the vision*. I wouldn't have to pay any rent, just take care of the maintenance. Deacon Proctor called me later to confirm the job and the offer of the house.

I believe God was deliberately taking me out of Philadelphia. I wasn't growing in Him while I was there. Every time I shared with the people in my church the vision I had to work with the homeless, they thought a crazy man had come back from Puerto Rico. I realized that many people in my church wanted material possessions more than they wanted to accomplish God's will. Several didn't even want to be around me. If I saw any of the church members doing something I knew wasn't godly, I would tell them about it, showing them the Scriptures concerning what they were doing. As a result, people began to call me a "fanatic," and I frequently felt rejected in my own church. Now the Lord had opened a door for me to move away.

God Doesn't Want You Here!

I left Philadelphia and went to live in that house on the hill near Lansdale in Telford, Pennsylvania. This house, located on three acres of land, was like a little mansion — but a mansion that needed help! It appeared someone had begun to work on it but had never finished. I took the job at Longacres Chicken and Poultry, cleaning machines on the third shift, from 9:00 p.m. to 6:00 a.m. As I worked there, I knew this wasn't God's perfect will for my life! When I interviewed for the job with Arlin Lapp, a Christian from the Mennonite church, he told me "God didn't call you to come here to work. He has called you to be in full-time ministry." By this point, I was completely fed up. I had no money and couldn't pay my bills.

"Give me a check every week," I replied, "and I'll go out there and preach."

"Joey, I'm going to give you the job, but remember God doesn't want you here!"

After two months of working at Longacres, I felt spiritually dried up. I couldn't go out to the streets to preach anymore because of the hours I had to work. Knowing I couldn't take any more of this, I found a job at Seaboard Automotive. My wages there were three dollars an hour less, but I didn't care. I just wanted to be out in the streets preaching again. The hours at Seaboard allowed me to do that. Not too long after, my friend Efrain Cotto told me a church in Kennett Square, Pennsylvania, needed a substitute pastor for a while. The current pastor had had a nervous breakdown, and the church needed someone to take her place while she recovered. Efrain asked me if I would be willing to fill in. I was ready to do *anything* for the Lord so I told him I would take the job.

The church had about twenty people in it at the time. In addition to preaching on Sunday's, every Friday when I got off work, I went to Kennett Square and held meetings at the mushroom farms among the Mexican immigrants who worked there. Most of them accepted Jesus as their Savior. I was still selling clothes on the side, and sometimes after the meetings, I would open the trunk of the car and start selling low-priced clothing to the people to whom I had just been preaching! After about two months, Efrain told me the pastor was doing much better and would be resuming her responsibilities at the Kennett Square Church. By the time I left that church, it had grown from 20 to around 60 members. Many of the new members were people who had been saved in the street meetings.

I had decided to go back to Philadelphia when I met Pastor John Yamin from Quakertown, Pennsylvania. Someone had told him about me, and he wanted to meet me. I began visiting his church and sensed this was where the Lord wanted me. I was accepted by the leadership there, and they acknowledged me as the evangelist of their church. Whenever I wasn't preaching outside the area, I would be at my local church in Quakertown hearing the Word of God —

Pastor Yamin was a very good teacher. When he first started his church, he had only 10 to 15 people in it. Over time his congregation had grown to around 150.

God Opens New Doors

I went back to see Glen Alderfer who was now pastoring Towamencin Mennonite Church and told him I wanted to do a big crusade for the young people in the Telford area. Glen thought it was a great idea and supported me every way he could. We found a few young girls from his church who wanted to help, and I made them the crusade secretaries. These three girls, along with one young man, began typing letters for me to mail to the other local churches. I didn't have the money for postage, but the Lord always provided. I just kept trusting and believing Him.

We held the rally at Franconia Mennonite Church, a good-sized facility with a seating capacity of 800. About 600 people came out, and 13 or 14 people were saved that night. Many of the people who came to the rally had never heard a preacher like me. I was *loud!* One elderly man in the congregation came up to me afterward and told me he had been in that church for years and always needed to use his hearing aid to hear the message. However when I spoke, he had to take his hearing aid *out of his ear* because I was so loud. Even without it, he understood me perfectly. Glen Alderfer really laughed when he heard that!

That same night a brother named Jerry Cardona came up to me and asked if I had my testimony on tape. I told him I didn't, but I knew the message had been recorded that night. He explained that some of his friends, who owned a supermarket, had a tape-duplicating machine of their own. If I wanted, I could buy blank tapes and ask to use the machine to duplicate them. That way, I not only would have my testimony on tape, but I could generate income for my ministry through tape sales. I met Jerry's friend Paul Landis, who was a really energetic guy. He was enthusiastic about serving the Lord—just fired up for Jesus. Paul introduced me to his wife Mary, and they invited Jerry Cardona and me to have lunch with them sometime. Paul also introduced me to his brother Donald, the one who actually owned the duplicating machine. I asked Don if I could use it to duplicate my testimony tape, and he said yes.

I bought a number of blank tapes and began duplicating cassettes of my testimony. As I traveled preaching the Word of God, the tape sales were a blessing. Don and his family also helped me in other ways. His mother felt moved by the Lord to buy me new sound equipment because Glen and I needed better equipment in order to hold street meetings in Philadelphia. Despite their good-heartedness, I really didn't understand these people, and in some ways, it was hard for them to understand me! They were so kind and loving that sometimes I thought they were trying to con me and "get over on me" just as people had done to me in the past. I couldn't comprehend why they were doing so much to help me because I still didn't know how to receive from others. Now I realize God was using them to bring healing in this area of my life. I continued to travel further and further, going to New York, Connecticut, New Jersey, and to other states preaching the gospel. I held many meetings in Bethlehem, Pennsylvania, with Pastor John Yamin helping me coordinate the big crusades.

Chapter 26

He Who Finds a Wife

One day Paul Landis asked me if I was praying for a wife. I had been saved for about five years at the time, and I told him yes, I was praying for one but hadn't found anyone I felt strongly about in my heart. I had met many nice Christian women, but I thought they were too materialistic for me. They didn't seem to be seeking the direction of the Holy Spirit. Instead, all they talked about were beautiful homes and husbands with well-paid secular jobs. I knew I wasn't called to have a secular job; God had made it clear He had called me to full-time ministry.

Paul and Mary asked me if I wanted them to pray with me for a wife. They told me this was a special gift they had from the Lord. I started to laugh when I heard that because I had never heard of anyone having that kind of a gift! I let them pray anyway.

My "Fleece"

On my way to Philadelphia one day, I remembered talking recently to my sister Vivian about giving her some money to help with her bills. As I drove along Route 309 South, I began to think about the prayer Paul and Mary Landis had prayed for me to receive a wife. I said to myself, "Paul and his wife prayed for me, but I need to receive a sign from God just like Gideon's fleece." In the book of Judges, Gideon had asked the Lord for a sign to confirm if it was really God speaking to him to save Israel from the Midianite nation. Gideon put a wooly lamb's skin—a "fleece"—on the floor and asked God to cause the fleece to be dry the next morning even though the surrounding ground would be wet with dew. The Lord did this, and Gideon knew God was speaking to him to deliver his nation. I was trying to put out my own "fleece" by asking God to give me a sign to let me know which woman He had chosen as my wife.

My sister Vivian worked at Kensington Hospital. "Lord," I prayed, "Vivian works with a woman named Monica. I'm asking you to remove Monica from her job and give her a better one somewhere else. I'm also asking you to replace Monica with the woman you've chosen for me. Vivian can introduce us, and that will be the sign she is to be my wife."

About a month later, Vivian told me her friend Monica had quit her job. I had already forgotten about the "fleece" I had put before the Lord, although I think He allowed it to happen this way. After another month, Vivian told me about a nice Christian girl, a quiet and sweet young woman, who had started working with her. Vivian wanted to introduce us to one another. Unfortunately, I had forgotten completely about the fleece!

Vivian called me one day because her car was in the garage; she needed me to pick her up at work and take her to get the car. I went to the hospital and spent some time talking to Vivian's friends, Valerie and Otilia. Valerie in particular was a beautiful black woman who really loved the Lord. I used to tease her because she was always dressed so well and was really elegant looking. That day as I was talking with Vivian's friends, I heard footsteps behind me. I turned around and saw the girl Vivian had been telling me about.

"She's Your Wife!"

As I looked at her, she suddenly stopped right in her tracks. She was holding a bunch of papers in her hands and just stood there looking at me. I mean, she *stared* at me for about ten seconds while I stared right back at her. Suddenly, the Lord spoke to my heart, "That's your wife." I quickly rejected those thoughts because when I looked at her, even though she was very attractive, I didn't think she seemed spiritually "all there" with God. She walked toward us, and Vivian introduced her to me. Her name was Damaris Castro. I talked with her for a while before Vivian and I left to pick up the car. I kept wondering why God had told me *she* was going to be my wife!

About a month later Vivian wanted me to go with her to pay bills. When I arrived at the hospital to meet my sister, Damaris walked in once again with papers in her hands. For the second time, Damaris stared at me as she walked in. And for the second time, the Lord told me she was going to be my wife. I didn't like any of this because I felt Damaris was spiritually "empty." When I looked at her, I couldn't see Christ at the center of her life. Despite this, she was an extremely nice, quiet young woman with a gentle spirit. When she first spoke to me, I had thought she was from another country because of her heavy accent. I soon learned she had been born and raised in Puerto Rico but had moved to the United States when she was thirteen years old.

As we continued to talk, Damaris told me she had just finished four years of college and had a Bachelor's degree in education. At this point, I really wasn't interested in talking with her anymore because no matter what the Lord told me, I just couldn't see myself with her. I was relieved when Vivian said she was ready to leave.

Not That Girl!

I happened to be looking for someone who could translate my testimony tract from English to Spanish. I thought about my good friend Johnny Alvarado in Puerto Rico and also about my cousin Maribel. Unfortunately, both Johnny and Maribel used too many "educated" words, and the translation of the tract not only *didn't* sound like me, it ended up sounding like an "educated" gangster! Because of that, I wanted to find someone who would translate the tract in a way that would still "sound like" me. The Lord told me to get Damaris Castro to do it. I immediately told Him, "Lord! Anyone else, but *not that girl!*"

One day I went to see Vivian at the hospital, and Damaris was working in the same area. I just said a quick "hi" to her, and that was it. I handed something to Vivian, and as I was walking away, I stopped, turned around, and asked Damaris if she could do me a favor.

"I remember you told me you can translate from English to Spanish. I have my testimony tract in English, and I'm looking for someone to translate it. Can you do it for me?"

Damaris was enthusiastic as she told me she really enjoyed doing things like that. I told her I was going to pay her because "I don't want you to do anything free for me."

Damaris, however, did not agree and kept telling me I didn't have to pay her. I replied firmly that I was going to pay her *anyway*. She finished translating the tract in about three days, and I figured I already knew how this was going to work. I would tell her I was going to pay her, and she would say, "No." Then, I'd invite her to dinner, she'd say "no" the first time — and I'd leave it at that!

When Vivian called me to tell me the tract was done, I went to pick it up. After I arrived at the hospital, Damaris showed me everything she had done with it. After she finished, I told her I was going to give her $40 for it. She said no, she didn't want the money. So I said, "Well, I'll take you out to dinner. Is that all right?"

I was hoping, of course, she'd say no to that too. However, to my surprise and horror, she said yes. I thought, "Oh great! What in the world have I gotten myself into?" I liked Damaris well enough, but I questioned why God would tell me she was going to be my wife. This I simply could not understand.

The First Date

We made a date for Saturday night. When I picked her up, I only had $10 in my pocket so I took her to Roy Rogers. I bought myself a cup of coffee and got her some chicken. As Damaris started to read the tract to me in her gentle voice, I began to really like the sweet spirit I sensed within her. Unfortunately, I became extremely uncomfortable around her because I was anxious I would hear those words again in my heart — "she's going to be your wife." I took her home, and she asked me if I wanted to come in. I told her I couldn't, I had things to do. Before Damaris got out of the car, I asked her what church she attended. She told me she had been going to a Baptist church on 7th and Erie Avenue. I mentioned I knew the pastor there. I left out the part that while some of my friends wanted me to preach there, the Baptist pastor wasn't too happy with my Pentecostal doctrine!

After Damaris told me about her church, she confided she had stopped going there and was now going to the International Assembly of God Church. She felt she had been "missing out" in the other church. As I looked into her eyes, I noticed they were filled with tears — I thought for a moment I had done something wrong. I asked her if she was okay, and she said yes. Then she added, "You know, there was something about your tract that really touched me. I accepted the Lord Jesus when I was 12 years old. I've been going to church for about 12 years now [she was 24 years old at the time], but I feel I'm not really free."

"When I read the part in your tract that said, 'I'm free! I'm free! I'm free!' my body started to tremble, and I haven't been able to sleep for the past three days."

I didn't know my tract would have such an impact on this girl's life! She continued, "I love Jesus, and I want to do more for God."

233

Looking at Damaris, I felt a desire in my heart to help her out.

"Look if you want me to help you grow spiritually, I'll be glad to do so, but don't start developing any romantic feelings toward me! Whatever you do, do not misinterpret my friendship for love!"

I told her if she wanted, I would take her to visit my church in Quakertown the next morning, and she agreed to go with me. Then I asked her if I could give her something; she looked at me in surprise. I gave her a hug, and as soon as I did, I felt the presence of God. I told her, however, I only wanted to be her friend, and added, "Maybe you can help me out by typing letters for me — I could use a secretary in my ministry." Damaris said she'd be glad to — she liked helping out that way.

That night I stayed at Vivian's house. I was still living in Telford, but since I was going to take Damaris to church with me the next morning, I stayed at my sister's. Sunday morning I picked Damaris up, and she brought her nephew with her. We drove to Quakertown, and as soon as we walked into the church together, everyone turned to look at us. Pastor Yamin grabbed my hand, and after I had introduced her to him, he said, "Some friend you got there, Joe! She's real pretty!" I replied she was *only a friend.*

Damaris really liked our church. Pastor Yamin prayed for her after the service, and she came out of the building with a new glow on her face — it was the joy of the Lord. As the days passed, she began to be a great help to me, typing letters and doing whatever needed to be done. Every now and then, I would take her to different churches with me so she could help me with the tapes. Whenever I had a crusade, she helped me create the flyers.

Something in my heart was growing toward Damaris, and I was getting more nervous around her every day! I didn't know if I should break off the friendship we had. Of course, I didn't remember that prayer I had prayed to God on Route 309.

Meeting the Family

Eventually Damaris invited me to her house, and I met her mother, Hilda, a woman of very strong character, and her two sisters. Her brother Willie came down from New York another time, and I met him too. Her older sister Carmen and I were comfortable and relaxed with each other, but her other sister, Awilda, was much more serious in nature and not as easy for me to get to know. Damaris also had some very pretty little nieces and handsome nephews, and they really liked it when I came around. I spent time talking with them about Jesus, and sometimes Damaris and I took them to church with us.

As time passed, that "something" in my heart was growing stronger toward Damaris, and I began to be anxious and bothered by it all. One evening we were talking as I left her house. Everyone else was upstairs, and Damaris had to go to work the next day. She had stopped working at Kensington Hospital and found another job at M. Cardone Industries. Getting ready to leave, I gave her a hug and a kiss on the cheek — and she told me she had begun to have very strong feelings for me. Hearing this really upset me — almost made me angry — although I didn't let her know. Even though this wasn't what I thought "should" happen, I was feeling something similar toward her too.

When I got into my car, the Holy Spirit told me to just love Damaris, but I kept battling it. The "emptiness" I had sensed in her was the biggest problem for me.

"Lord," I said, "if this is the woman You have for me, You will have to fill her with your Holy Spirit."

After praying that prayer, I began to notice all of her good qualities, and I saw she was becoming a big help to me in my ministry. One day while we were talking, she told me how she used to feel when she was going to the Baptist Church. She often felt out of place and rejected. I could see she was really hurting inside.

The next day I called her up and told her I wouldn't be coming to the city for the next three days; there was something I wanted to fast and pray about. Even though I didn't want to accept it, my feelings were growing stronger toward her every day. Everyone who saw me with her just smiled although they didn't say a word. I had already told the Lord if *anyone* said *anything* to me about her, I would end my friendship with her. And so *no one* said *anything* to me about Damaris Castro. Even the Landis family did not say anything — all they did was smile! And Glen Alderfer obviously thought highly of her too. He always asked me how she was doing, but otherwise, he never mentioned her to me.

Filled With His Spirit

After fasting for three days, I called Damaris. I told her I was going to take her to work that morning at 9:00 a.m. As soon as she opened the door, I laid my hands on her and began to pray.

"Father God, fill this girl with your Holy Spirit."

As soon as I spoke, her whole body began to shake as the power of God came upon her. She started to weep, the tears running down her face. Damaris said she didn't know what was happening to her — but I knew it was the power of God resting upon her. After a while, she went back upstairs to wash her face, and when she came back down, I saw that glow on her countenance once more.

One evening I picked up Damaris, my sister Evelyn, and a couple of other people to go to 20th and Tasker to hold a street meeting. After we arrived, Damaris and I remained in the car talking. After a few minutes, I asked her to get out of the car for a little while; I wanted to be alone to meditate on God's Word before it was time for me to preach.

Upon stepping out of the car, it was like a big cloud covered the entire vehicle. I couldn't even hear the people outside. I could see them, but that was about it. Suddenly, the Lord brought back to my remembrance the "fleece" I had put before Him when I was driving on Route 309. He reminded me of the prayer that Paul and Mary Landis had prayed and my own specific prayer that the Lord would remove Monica and put a girl in her place who would become my wife. *That girl was Damaris.* There had already been a few times I was ready to cut off our friendship because I felt I was "having problems" with her. The "problem" wasn't Damaris, however. It was me. I was afraid. I had never really known how to love someone, and what I was feeling for her was so strong it frightened me.

Chapter 27

Damaris, God's Choice!

That night after the service was over, I took Damaris home. For the last nine months I had kept telling her *not* to fall in love with me, that we were only friends. When we arrived at her house about 10:00 p.m., I told her we needed to talk. We sat at her kitchen table, and I blurted out, "You know what? You are my wife!" Her eyes became enormous as she asked, *"What do you mean?"* I told her I knew she was the girl God had chosen for me.

God had already told me He had a wife for me — and He also let me know I didn't have to go out looking for her. At one time, I had thought He was going to bring my ex-girlfriend Carmen back into my life, but when I ran into her about nine months after I was saved, I no longer felt anything for her. That had really surprised me.

I continued to explain to Damaris, "I have never felt for anyone what I feel for you." I told her about the "fleece" I had set before the Lord, asking Him to remove Monica from her job and replace her with the girl who would become my wife. After I said all this to her, I gave her a big hug — and a kiss!

Confirmation

The next day when I went to pick her up at her job, she began to confirm what I had said to her the night before.

"Joey, I didn't need that job at Kensington Hospital. I already had a good job. I went to the interview just to stop my girlfriend from bugging me any more about it. There were two other candidates who were more qualified than I was for the position. And I needed references, but I didn't have any. One of the doctors saw me filling out my

238

application. When he asked my girlfriend who I was, she said I was a friend who was applying for the open position but I needed someone to give me a reference. The doctor told her he would be glad to provide one for me. He went straight to the personnel office where he gave me a good reference.

"When I left the office, the head of personnel told me, 'We'll call you if anything comes up, but we already have two other applicants more qualified for this position.' I didn't care too much about it anyway. I already had a good job, and I wasn't interested in this one. That was about 9:30 in the morning. When I arrived home at noon, the director of personnel at Kensington Hospital called to tell me I had the job! He told me he really didn't understand why he was giving it to me, but he felt he *had to*. So Joey, I agree with you. I think God really has put us together!" That very day I asked her to be my girlfriend, and I started taking her to my preaching engagements more often. We went to Charlie Keller's house in Quakertown one day. He and his family used to go to my church, and Charlie and his wife Mary had a tremendous love in their hearts for homeless children. Every time you turned around, Charlie had someone new at his house. They were like a big brother and sister to me.

A Battle Within

I was once again fighting fear and having thoughts about just cutting Damaris loose. I had so many problems, and I was scared to fall in love. My heart of stone had become a real heart of flesh; I didn't want to marry the wrong woman and mess up God's plan for my life, not to mention hurting her. For all these reasons, I was putting Damaris through a lot. She was never the problem — the problem was always me.

Another obstacle was the anger I continued to carry in my heart toward my mother. I believed I saw a number of qualities in Damaris that reminded me of her. Sometimes I'd get really upset at Damaris, and she'd wonder why. At other times, I didn't even want her to sit next to me! The Lord showed me I hadn't forgiven my mother. After being saved for nearly six years, I still had terrible resentment toward her. I even told Damaris one day I was still angry with my mother for the way she had treated me. I confessed to her the Lord told me to let go of the bitterness within.

A Word From God

I went to my mother. I asked her to forgive me for the hostility in my heart, telling her I forgave her for the way she had treated me when I was younger. I knew I had to do this because the Lord had told me if I got married with this unforgiveness in my heart, I would create all kinds of problems in my marriage.

That day at Charlie Keller's house, the Holy Spirit directed him to speak with me. He walked over, looked straight into my eyes, and said, "I'm going to tell you something. God is giving this girl to you, and He has told me to tell you to set a date to marry her. He is going to bless this marriage. This is the woman God is giving you and until you join your life with hers, you're going to continue to have the same problems you've been battling. You're probably thinking about just letting her go because the devil is attacking you. When the two of you become one, your prayer life will become even stronger, and those attacks will come to an end."

I was amazed to hear what Charlie said — I knew he had no idea what I was going through. That night I took Damaris back to Philadelphia. The following day I bought her an engagement ring and asked her to marry me. When I put the ring on her finger, the tears began to run down her face. I don't think she believed our relationship would ever make it that far! I asked her to tell her mother I was coming over the next day to talk to her about marrying her daughter.

Once again, I was scared. I had never done anything like this in my life. I had no idea what to say or how to act with her mother. However, I told Hilda I wanted to marry her daughter — we had already been dating for about a year and a half. She asked me if we had set a date, and I said yes. We wanted to get married on Damaris's birthday, January 26, 1986.

As soon as everyone found out we were engaged, they began to tell me, "Oh, I knew she was going to be your wife since the first day you walked into my house with her."

"The first day you walked into my church with her, God told me she was going to be your wife."

"I *knew* she was the woman for you!"

The Kind of Woman I Wanted

All of this was confirmation to me, and I began to have much more peace about marrying Damaris. However, the devil kept up the attack against us, trying to split us up because he knew once we were married, our prayer life would increase in power. Damaris had become a real "prayer warrior." Sometimes when I would call her house to talk to her, her nephew would tell me she was praying. There were times when I went to see her, and we'd be watching television. Suddenly, she'd turn to me and say, "Let's turn off the television and pray!" At first, I was surprised by this, but I realized this was just the kind of woman I had always wanted the Lord to give me — a woman who would put God first in her life. So we'd turn off the television and begin to pray. Her family was upstairs, but they *always* heard me because I *always* prayed loudly!

My mother was living in Puerto Rico and could not help with our wedding, but my father agreed to give me a couple of hundred dollars to help out with our expenses. I asked Glen Alderfer if we could use his church for the wedding and the reception even though their banquet hall only held around 200 people. He agreed. Glen had always told me, "When you get married, I want to have the privilege of marrying you!" He and I have become very good friends throughout the years, and he has helped me a great deal in the ministry. God has used him as an instrument to introduce me to so many people who still support our ministry today.

Chapter 28

God Plans a Wedding

The Lord started to really put everything together for us. First, a Christian sister blessed Damaris by making her wedding dress. Then, Marian Masland, the owner of my house in Telford, wanted us to live there after our marriage. I started to fix the house up and brought a group of young people who had been saved in our street meetings — Patricia whom we called Leti, her brother Carlos, and a few of his friends — to help me work on it. Sometimes Damaris's mom Hilda and her sister Carmen would come up to give us a hand as I spent nearly $4,000 getting the house ready for my bride.

You Are One!

The devil continued to come after me with everything he had. I didn't know how in the world I was going to support a wife. I asked the Lord to confirm to me if it was His will for Damaris to quit work and travel with me when I preached. Not long after praying that we went to see a friend of ours, Angel Roman, because we wanted him to videotape our wedding. When we walked into his house, Angelo's wife began to speak a prophetic word from the Holy Spirit to us.

"Joey, you are one person, and God provides for you! When you two get married, you'll *become* one, and God will *still* provide for *both* of you."

Although I was not expecting her to say this, I immediately felt the presence of God. That was confirmation to me that Damaris would be able to leave her job and work full-time in the ministry with me. I knew it was going to be hard for her. I had already spent six years in the ministry, and there were times that were very difficult, but God always showed Himself to be true and faithful. I knew God was going to make great provision for us.

More Than We Could Imagine

Charlie and Mary, and their son Chuck were set to cater all the food for our wedding reception. There was one minor problem: *I didn't have any money.* Everything I had purchased, I had bought in faith, trusting God that when it was time to pay for it, I would have the money. I even rented my tuxedo by faith. A week before the wedding, God began to provide finances miraculously. Since people knew I was getting married soon, they started calling me to come by their houses or businesses to pick up "something we have for you." When I arrived, they would give me $100, $200, $400 for the wedding. Even my father called me to help out some more!

We had invited somewhere between 150 to 200 people, but when our wedding day arrived, about 500 people showed up. We didn't even know who half these people were! Many of my friends flew in from Puerto Rico, including Eliezer Espinosa and his family, and pastors and other friends of mine drove down from New York.

At our reception, people continued to bless us with gifts. Even though we had only planned food for about 225 people, God miraculously stretched it to feed over 500! People had to sit on the stairs because there was just no room in the banquet hall. There were musical groups singing at our reception — and we didn't even know who they were, but they sounded great. It was a true blessing to see the mighty hand of God move to take care of all the details of our wedding.

We had been blessed with two round-trip plane tickets to Florida with all expenses paid for our honeymoon. And not only were we given the tickets for Florida, we even received tickets to fly from Florida to Puerto Rico right after our honeymoon week in order to hold two weeks of street meetings there. In addition to all this, we were blessed with over $4,000 in cash and all kinds of gifts to furnish our home.

Early the next morning after our wedding, Damaris and I went to my father's house so he could take us to the airport. Once we arrived in Puerto Rico after our Florida honeymoon, we spent the next two weeks with my mother since she had not been able to make it to the wedding. We were holding street meetings in the area in which she lived, and she was excited to see how God was blessing our ministry. My mother loved Damaris dearly, and I was blessed to see how well the two of them got along. After we finished the crusade, several pastors indicated they wanted me to come back to Puerto Rico. I told them I would return in October of that year. When I returned, I got in contact with Manny for the first time in three years! It was a joy to share with him what God was doing in our ministry and how He was blessing it.

The Rest of Our Story

Damaris and I had only been married for three weeks when my sister Vivian called me at my mother's house in Puerto Rico. She told me that Marian Masland, the owner of our house in Telford, had died. That brought such sadness to my heart because I had really come to like Marian. Upon our return to Philadelphia, we began to look for another place to live because Marian's family wanted to sell the property.

That same year, we incorporated our ministry, naming it Worldwide Evangelistic Ministries, Inc. Damaris and I continued to travel all over the United States, Puerto Rico, and the Dominican Republic holding street meetings. Two and a half years later, Damaris became pregnant with our first child, Christine Lynette. In 1989, we were inspired by the Lord to start a church in a building that had been donated to us. We raised the funds to renovate it, and when we were done, we ended up buying the other two houses adjacent to that building to start a men's recovery home.

A year later, five more buildings adjacent to each other were donated to our ministry, and the Lord blessed us with the finances to renovate those as well, in order to house mothers with children, and single girls who were seeking recovery from drug and alcohol addiction. When our daughter Christine was twelve years old, the Lord blessed us with our second daughter, Ivellise Joy, who was born in 2001. As of today, we are still holding street meetings all over the United States. We have visited many other countries to hold seminars and are still pressing on toward our vision of having a larger place of worship, a Christian academy, and a Bible institute. In all of this, we have seen God's hand of provision and blessing, and we continue to say...

"...the glory goes to the Lord Jesus Christ and to Him alone!"

Dear Friend,

If you would like to be free from your sins and live a happy life, give Jesus Christ the opportunity. The Bible tells us in John 8:32, "You will know the truth, and the truth will set you free." In John 14:14 there is another promise from God for us: "If you ask anything in my name, I will do it."

Friend, you have to confess your sins to be born again of the Spirit. Ask Jesus Christ the Son of the Living God to come into your heart right now. He loves you and is waiting for you to cry out to Him. God Bless You!

If you are interested in a DVD or CD of this testimony, all you need to do is call our office for more details.

Please call

Worldwide Evangelistic Ministries, Inc.

Main office

(215) 223-1022

(215) 223- 1916

Special Thanks

I want to give a special thanks to the following people and to those too numerous to mention here, who have made this book possible.

Mr. Ruben and Jill Tarno

Mr. Fred and Joanne Newfield

Rev. Donald and Kathleen Landis

The Landis Supermarket family

Dr. Mason Beale

Mr. George and Pauline Young

Mr. Louis Borelli

Mr. Jack and Lynn Kreischer and their daughter Jennifer

Mr. Robert and Lynn Weber

Mr. Roger and Miriam Tarno

Mr. Anthony and Judy DePaul

Mr. John and Elsie Jo Cardone

Mr. Michael and Delores Johnston